THE ELIJAH DOCTRINE

Chronicle_2 – 2nd Phase of the Cryptex puzzle

Written by Elijah H. Bennett

The son of Olivia

"THE PATH OF THE SIGN"

The Elijah Doctrine Chronicles is a complete and accurate decoding of the Bible. The scriptures used in the work are of the NIV (New International Version) translation.

ISBN – 978-0-692-08177-8

THE INSTRUCTIONS

2ND Phase of the cryptex puzzle

(Note: Each scriptural verse represents a revealing clue! Thus, the revelations revealed by them are much like tiny pieces of a revealing puzzle!)

(Note2: There are three phases of the cryptext puzzle buried within the Holy Bible. The three phases consist of three challenging tests that must be overcome. The three tests are as follows: The test of Superstition, The test of Fear, and The test of Ideology. Each of the three phases will be revealed by the revelations uncovered from the base decoder. The base decoder is the building block that will enable you to decipher and understand the mysteries of the scriptures. The more revelations you uncover; the more the base decoder will be expanded revealing each phase of the cryptex puzzle. The building block for the base decoder will be displayed by the following symbol (=). This symbol (=) when not used in a mathematic equation will represent a "correspondence too." For example: (x = x) will represent the following: ("x" corresponds to "x"))

The goal in the 2nd phase of the cryptex puzzle is to overcome: **[The test of Fear]**

Welcome to the Elijah Doctrine!

INTRODUCTION

In the *1st Chronicle* of the Elijah Doctrine, you discovered how (Four prominent horns) corresponded to the following revelations:

- **{1ST prominent horn}** = [4TH head = 4TH hill = 4TH king] = [4th star = 4th spirit before his throne = 4th angel blasting 4th trumpet] = [4th priest *(blowing trumpet)* = Harps = 4th man = 4th elder of Judah = 4th golden lampstand] = [1ST beast = lion = 1ST living creature = like a lion = 1ST cherubim = 1ST chariot = Brown horses = 1ST spirit = 1ST angel = North = 1st wind of the earth = 1st wind of heaven *(churning up the great sea)* = 1ST guard of the city = 1ST apocalyptic rider *(Its rider held a bow)* = Brown horses = 1ST swift messenger = Peals of thunder] = [1ST kingdom = Element of Gold = Fall of the Egyptian dynasty]

- **{2ND prominent horn}** = [5TH head = 5TH hill = 5TH king] = [5th star = 5th spirit before his throne = 5th angel blasting 5th trumpet] = [5th priest *(blowing trumpet)* = cymbals = 5th man = 5th elder of Judah = 5th golden lampstand] = [2ND beast = bear = 2ND living creature = like an ox = 2ND cherubim = 2ND chariot = Black horses = 2ND spirit = 2ND angel = South = 2nd wind of the earth = 2nd wind of heaven *(churning up the great sea)* = 2ND guard of the city = 2ND apocalyptic rider *(Its rider was holding a pair of scales in his hand)* = Black horses = 2ND swift messenger = Rumblings] = [2ND kingdom = Element of Silver = Fall of the Babylonian and Assyrian dynasties]

- **{3RD prominent horn}** = [6TH head = 6TH hill = 6TH king] = [6th star = 6th spirit before his throne = 6th angel blasting 6th trumpet] = [6th priest *(blowing trumpet)* = Lyres = 6th man = 6th elder of Judah = 6th golden lampstand] = [3RD beast = leopard = 3RD living creature = face like a man = 3RD cherubim = 3RD chariot = Pale horses = 3RD spirit = 3RD angel = West = 3rd wind of the earth = 3rd wind of heaven *(churning up the great sea)* = 3RD guard of the city = 3RD apocalyptic rider *(to kill by sword, famine and plague)* = Pale horses = 3RD swift messenger = Flashes of lightning] = [3RD kingdom = Element of Bronze = Fall of the Persian and Nubian dynasties]

- **{4TH prominent horn}** = [7TH head = 7TH hill = 7TH king *(And he was given a great sword)*] = [7th star = 7th spirit before his throne = 7th angel blasting 7th trumpet] = [7th priest *(blowing trumpet)* = shouts = 7th man = 7th elder of Judah] = [7th golden lampstand = 7th church] = [4TH beast *(The beast and the ten horns you saw)* = Beast coming out of the sea *(ancient serpent)* = Scarlet beast *(devil)* = Red dragon *(Satan)*] = [Satan *(name of a man)* = Mighty angel *(coming up from the east)* = *Who is worthy to break the seals and open the scroll?* 4TH living creature = like a flying eagle = 4TH cherubim = 4TH chariot = Fiery red horses = 4TH spirit = 4TH angel = East = 4th wind of the earth = 4th wind of heaven *(churning up the great sea)* = 4TH guard of the city = 4TH apocalyptic rider *(To him was given a large sword)* = Fiery red horses = 4TH swift messenger = Earthquake] = [Then I saw the beast and the kings of the earth and their armies gathered together to make war against the rider on the horse and his army] = [4th kingdom = Element of Iron = Fall of the Greek dynasty]

In this *2nd Chronicle* you will discover how these four prominent horns also reveal another important revelation!

For example: The four prominent horns also correspond to the following four gospels:

- [The Gospel of Mathews]
- [The Gospel of Mark]
- [The Gospel of Luke]
- [The Gospel of John]

Contrary to what is widely taught throughout the world, these four gospels are not four separate books written from the accounts of four different authors. The four gospels collectively represent one complete puzzle. Hidden within the enigma of this puzzle contains the sacred document of Immanuel, which foretells the exact accounting regarding the lives of Jesus the Nazarene, John the son of Zechariah, and the disciples. The true accounting is different from what is written, believed, foretold, and taught. There is also a great revelation that will be revealed regarding the Knights Templars.

There are seven challenging tests that must be completed within this phase of the puzzle. Each test will correspond to one of seven miraculous signs that must be uncovered. You must unveil the existence of seven woes hidden behind each of the seven miraculous signs to reveal the mystery. To begin, you must start by forging together the four gospels: Matthew, Mark, Luke, and John, into one complete book. In this stage of the puzzle, you must train your eyes to see what lays hidden beneath the surfaces of the Scriptures, and to the many traps that await you!

The revelation you are about to uncover will unveil the true meaning behind these words, "There is nothing concealed that will not be disclosed or hidden that will not be made known" – Luke 12:2

THE

2ND EXODUS PERIOD

CHAPTER ONE- 2ND PHASE OF THE CRYPTEX PUZZLE- THE PATH OF THE SIGN

The first test in this Chapter is to unveil the mystery revealed behind the [1st woe] by revealing the revelations concealed behind the 1st miraculous sign: [**The place and birth of Jesus**]

(Note: To uncover this mystery, you must begin by revealing the unseen revelations regarding Joseph, Mary, Zechariah and Elizabeth! To start, you must begin by following the Path of Joseph and Mary)

THE PATH OF JOSEPH AND MARY

The first thing you must do is look closely at the bold portion in the following two descriptions below,

Luke 2:4-5 – [**So Joseph also went up from the town of Nazareth in Galilee to Judea, to Bethlehem the town of David,** because **he belonged to the house and line of David.** He went there to register with Mary, who was pledged to be married to him and was expecting a child]

Luke 1:26-27 – [**In the sixth month, God sent the angel Gabriel to Nazareth, a town in Galilee, to a virgin pledged to be married** to a man named **Joseph, a descendant of David. The virgin's name was Mary**]

The next thing you must do is remove the following descriptions from the verses.

1- So Joseph also went up from the town of Nazareth in Galilee to Judea
2- God sent the angel Gabriel to Nazareth, a town in Galilee, to a virgin pledged to be married
3- because he belonged to the house and line of David
4- In the sixth mouth

(Note: The following four descriptions above reveal four major clues. To reveal them you must examine each of the four descriptions above)

Next, re-list the following description removed from the verses.

- [So Joseph also went up from the town of Nazareth in Galilee to Judea]

(Note2: This description is written deceptively and reveals a vital clue. To uncover the clue, you must reveal two hidden clues that are hidden behind the two region lands. For example: The following description 'from the town of Nazareth in Galilee to Judea' are two regions that correspond to two separate lands (two of which do not associate with one another). Example2: One of the following two regions (Nazareth or Judea) correspond to the land of the Gentiles, the other, the land of the Jews.)

Here is the first question. In which land referring to the [(*eastern hill country*) and (*western hill country*)] does the town of Nazareth correspond to?

(Note3: The town of Nazareth is symbolic and corresponds to the region known as Nazareth (also known as a region in the descendant land of Ephraim). This region represents a region in the land of the eastern hill country as representing the descendants of Esau (See the 1st Chronicle for more detail regarding the nation of Esau))

Here is the clue: The town of Nazareth corresponds to the region of Nazareth and represents a region in the following land of the eastern hill country: [The Land of Samaria *(also known as the land of the Gentiles)*]!

The next thing you must do is bring back the revelation revealed in the 1st Chronicle of the Elijah Doctrine regarding the Nation of Esau and merge the revelations together regarding the descendants of Esau (also known as the descendant land of Ephraim), the eastern hill country, to reflect the events that proceeds after the 2nd exodus, into the correct context as seen below,

- {Nation of Esau} = {Ten Horns} = [Ten kings = Ten tribes: *(Ephraim, Manasseh, Naphtali, Dan, Asher, Issachar, Zebulon, Simeon, Reuben, and Gad)* = Nation of Ephraim = *who are yet to receive a kingdom of their own* = Kingdom of Samaria = Conquered by the Assyrian Empire = Exodus by the Kushite Empire *(Wadi of Egypt)*] = [2nd Exodus] = **{Descendants of Esau} = {Eastern hill country} = {Land of Samaria} = {Land of the Gentiles} = [Region of Nazareth]**

Here is the next question. In what land referring to the [(*eastern hill country*) and (*western hill country*)] does the region of Judea correspond to?

(Note4: The region of Judea corresponds to the land of the Jews (also known as the descendant land of Judah). This region represents a region in the land of the western hill country as representing the descendants of Jacob (See the 1st Chronicle for more detail regarding the Nation of Jacob))

Here is the next clue: Judea corresponds to the region called Judea and represents a region in the following land of the western hill country: [The Land of Jerusalem *(also known as the land of the Jews)*]!

The next thing you must do is bring back the revelation revealed in the 1st Chronicle of the Elijah Doctrine regarding the Nation of Jacob and merge the revelations together regarding the descendants of Jacob (also known as the descendant land of Judah), the western hill country, to reflect the events that proceeds after the 2nd exodus, into the correct context as seen below,

- {Nation of Esau} = {Ten Horns} = [Ten kings = Ten tribes: *(Ephraim, Manasseh, Naphtali, Dan, Asher, Issachar, Zebulon, Simeon, Reuben, and Gad)* = Nation of Ephraim = *who are yet to receive a kingdom of their own* = Kingdom of Samaria = Conquered by the Assyrian Empire = Exodus by the Kushite Empire *(Wadi of Egypt)*] = [2nd Exodus] = {Descendants of Esau} = {Eastern hill country} = {Land of Samaria} = {Land of the Gentiles} = [Region of Nazareth]

- {Nation of Jacob} = {Beast} = [single tribe: *(Benjamin)* = Nation of Judah = *remained in the city* = Conquered by Babylonian Empire = Exodus by the Persian Empire] = [2nd Exodus] = [Kingdom of Jerusalem] = **{Descendants of Jacob}** = **{Western hill country}** = **{Land of Jerusalem}** = **{Land of the Jews}** = **[Region of Judea]**

Here is the next question. In which region referring to Nazareth and Judea does Joseph natively correspond to?

(Note5: To reveal Joseph native region you must locate the next clue in the third description removed from the verses)

Next, re-list the following description removed from the verses.

- [because he belonged to the house and line of David]

(Note6: This description reveals a hidden clue. For example: The house and line of David does not represent the City of David (nor does it correspond to the bloodline of David). The house and line of David represents the descendants of Judah (from the Nation of Judah who remained in the City of David before taken into captivity to the land of Babylon), and corresponds to the land of the western hill country, known as the land of Jerusalem (established after the 2ⁿᵈ exodus, when the Nation of Judah, move on from the land from which they were taken))

Here is the next clue: Joseph *(a native Jew)* corresponds to the house and line of David *(descendant of Judah)* and is natively from the following region of the western hill country: [The region of Judea]!

(Note7: Joseph does not go up from the town of Nazareth in Galilee to the region of Judea because Nazareth represents a region in the land of the eastern hill country, the land of the Gentiles (land of Samaria), and Joseph is natively from the land of the western hill country, the land of the Jews (land of Jerusalem))

(Note8: The following two lands: land of the Jews (descendants of Jacob) and the land of the Gentiles (descendants of Esau) did not associate with one another (remained in conflict). This revelation corresponds to the following description 'You are well aware that it is against our law for a Jew to associate with or visit a Gentile' – Acts 10:28. This revelation also corresponds to the following description regarding the non-association with Jews and Samaritans '"You are a Jew," said the woman. "How can You ask for a drink from me, a Samaritan woman?" (For Jews do not associate with Samaritans – John 4:9))

The next thing you must do is merge the revelations together into the correct context as seen below,

- {Nation of Esau} = {Ten Horns} = [Ten kings = Ten tribes: *(Ephraim, Manasseh, Naphtali, Dan, Asher, Issachar, Zebulon, Simeon, Reuben, and Gad)* = Nation of Ephraim = *who are yet to receive a kingdom of their own* = Kingdom of Samaria = Conquered by the Assyrian Empire = Exodus by the Kushite Empire *(Wadi of Egypt)*] = [2nd Exodus] = {Descendants of Esau} = {Eastern hill country} = {Land of Samaria} = {Land of the Gentiles} = [Region of Nazareth]

- {Nation of Jacob} = {Beast} = [single tribe: *(Benjamin)* = Nation of Judah = *remained in the city* = Conquered by Babylonian Empire = Exodus by the Persian Empire] = [2nd Exodus] = [Kingdom of Jerusalem] = {Descendants of Jacob} = {Western hill country} = {Land of Jerusalem} = {Land of the Jews} = [Region of Judea: *(Joseph)*]

Next, re-list the following description removed from the verses.

- [God sent the angel Gabriel to Nazareth, a town in Galilee, to a virgin pledged to be married]

(Note9: This description is also written deceptively and reveals another major clue. For example: The town of Nazareth represents a region in the land of the Gentiles)

Here is the next question. In which native land referring to the [(*eastern hill country*) and (*western hill country*)] does Mary natively correspond to?

*(Note10: To reveal Mary's native region you must first uncover a hidden clue concealed by the revelation of Zechariah and Elizabeth. One of the clues is revealed behind this description **"In the sixth month!"** This revelation will be revealed shortly!)*

The next thing you must do is look closely at the bold portion in the following descriptions below,

Luke 1:5 - [In the time of Herod king of Judea there was a priest named **Zechariah,** who **belonged to the priestly division of Abijah**; his wife **Elizabeth was also a descendant of Aaron**]

Luke 1:23-24 - [When his time of service was completed, he returned home. After this his wife **Elizabeth became pregnant and for five months remained in seclusion**]

Luke 1:36 - [Even **Elizabeth your relative is going to have a child** in her old age, and **she who was said to be barren is in her sixth month**]

Luke 1:39-40 - [At that time **Mary got ready and hurried to a town in the hill country of Judea,** where she **entered Zechariah's home** and **greeted Elizabeth**]

Luke 1:56 - [**Mary stayed with Elizabeth** for about **three months and then returned home**]

Next, remove the following descriptions from the verses.

1- Zechariah belonged to the priestly division of Abijah; his wife Elizabeth was also a descendant of Aaron
2- Elizabeth your relative is going to have a child she who was said to be barren is in her sixth month
3- Mary hurried to a town in the hill country of Judea entered Zechariah's home greeted Elizabeth
4- Mary stayed with Elizabeth three months then returned home

The final thing you must do is bring back the following description.

5- [In the sixth month]

(Note11: To solve the mystery of Mary's native region you must locate a major clue revealed in the revelation of Zechariah and Elizabeth)

15

THE REVELATION OF ZECHARIAH AND ELIZABETH

Next, re-list the following description removed from the verses.

- [Zechariah belonged to the priestly division of Abijah; his wife Elizabeth was also a descendant of Aaron]

(Note12: The priestly division of Abijah corresponds to the priestly line of Aaron (thus, Aaron represents the father of the priestly division). This revelation corresponds to the following description 'But only you and your sons may serve as priests in connection with everything at the altar and inside the curtain. I am giving you the service of the priesthood as a gift. Anyone else who comes near the sanctuary is to be put to death.'– Numbers 18:7. The priestly line of Aaron also represents the house of Aaron that establishes the priestly line (thus, during the time of the 1st exodus, the Nation of Judah would maintain and preserve the priestly line of Aaron). This revelation corresponds to the following description 'Ephraim broke away from Judah'.– Isaiah 7:17. The priestly line of Aaron also corresponds to this description 'As for the priests, the descendants of Aaron, who lived on the farmlands around their towns or in any other towns, men were designated by name to distribute portions to every male among them and to all who were recorded in the genealogies of the Levites' – 2 Chronicles 31:19 (thus, after the 2nd exodus, the Land of Jerusalem would maintain and preserve the priestly line of Aaron))

(Note13: Zechariah belongs to the house and line of Aaron because he represents a descendant of Aaron and therefore belongs to the priestly division during the reign of Abijah (Thus, Abijah also a descendant of Aaron reigns as Lord over the land of Jerusalem and priestly division in the time of Joseph, Mary, Zechariah and Elizabeth). This revelation corresponds to the following description 'One day while Zechariah's division was on duty and he was serving as priest before God, he was chosen by lot, according to the custom of the priesthood, to enter the temple of the Lord' – Luke 1:8-9. This revelation also corresponds to this description 'This was to remind the Israelites that no one except a descendant of Aaron should come to burn incense before the LORD, or he would become like Korah and his followers' – Numbers 16:40. Elizabeth, on the other hand, also represents a descendant of Aaron (for she is the wife of a priest). She does not however, belong to the priestly division of Aaron (for she does not represent a Chief priest, High priest, or Levite). Her child, on the other hand, would continue the priestly line of Aaron for he would be born into the priestly division. This revelation corresponds to the following description 'The priest who is anointed and ordained to succeed his father as High priest is to make atonement. He is to put

16

on the sacred linen garments' – Leviticus 16:32. This revelation will be revealed in more detail moving forward)

Here is the next question. In what native region referring to the [(*eastern hill country*) and (*western hill country*)] does Zechariah and Elizabeth natively correspond to?

(Note14: There is a major clue revealed in one of the descriptions removed from the verses as well as a hidden clue revealed in the previous description of 2Chronicles 31:19)

Look closely at the following description below,

- [Mary hurried to a town in the hill country of Judea entered Zechariah's home greeted Elizabeth]

(Note15: Zechariah and Elizabeth (native Jews) are natively from a region in the western hill country land and resides outside of the city. The region of where both resides will reveal the meaning behind the bold part of this description **'As for the priests, the descendants of Aaron, who lived on the farmlands around their towns** *or in any other towns' - 2Chronicles 31:19)*

Here is the next clue: Zechariah and Elizabeth are natively from a region in the western hill country, the land of Jerusalem, and resides in the following area outside of the city and outside of the region of Judea: [The hill region of Judea].

The next thing you must do is merge the revelations together into the correct context.

- {Nation of Esau} = {Ten Horns} = [Ten kings = Ten tribes: *(Ephraim, Manasseh, Naphtali, Dan, Asher, Issachar, Zebulon, Simeon, Reuben, and Gad)* = Nation of Ephraim = *who are yet to receive a kingdom of their own* = Kingdom of Samaria = Conquered by the Assyrian Empire = Exodus by the Kushite Empire *(Wadi of Egypt)*] = [2ⁿᵈ Exodus] = {Descendants of Esau} = {Eastern hill country} = {Land of Samaria} = {Land of the Gentiles} = [Region of Nazareth]

- {Nation of Jacob} = {Beast} = [single tribe: *(Benjamin)* = Nation of Judah = *remained in the city* = Conquered by Babylonian Empire = Exodus by the Persian Empire] = [2ⁿᵈ Exodus] = [Kingdom of Jerusalem] = {Descendants of Jacob} = {Western hill country} = {Land of Jerusalem} = {Land of the Jews} = [**Hill region of Judea:** *(Zechariah and Elizabeth)*] = [Region of Judea: *(Joseph)*]

{**Important note:** The hill region of Judea *(land of the Jews)* that is located outside of the region called Judea, borders the region of Nazareth *(land of the Gentiles)*. This revelation will be revealed in more detail moving forward}

Next, re-list the following descriptions removed from the verses.

- Elizabeth your relative is going to have a child she who was said to be barren is in her sixth month
- Mary hurried to a town in the hill country of Judea entered Zechariah's home greeted Elizabeth
- Mary stayed with Elizabeth three months then returned home

- [In the sixth mouth]

(Note16: The following descriptions above reveal a major clue. For example: Mary and Elizabeth are blood relatives. However, Mary does not represent a descendant of Aaron (for she is not the wife, nor the daughter of a priest, nor will her child represent a descendant of Aaron, or continue the priestly line). Thus, Elizabeth represents the elder aunt of Mary (the elder sister of Mary's mother))

(Note17: Elizabeth was six months pregnant (after remaining in seclusion for five months). According to the account, Mary was visited by the angel Gabriel (she herself would conceive a child). From there, she would enter the home of Zechariah (the hill region of Judea) to greet Elizabeth and stay with her three months to witness the birth of her child (thus, upon returning home from the hill region of Judea, Mary is three months pregnant herself))

Here is the next clue: Mary *(a native Jew)* also corresponds to the house and line of David *(descendant of Judah)* and is natively from the following region land of the western hill country, the land of Jerusalem: [The region of Judea]!

(Note18: When Gabriel visited Mary, he did not go to a town in Galilee called Nazareth (also known as a region in the land of the Gentiles). Mary, a native Jew, does not represent a Nazarene or a native of Galilee from the land of Samaria (also known as a Galilean, Samaritan, or Gentile). Mary, like Joseph both belongs to the house and line of David (descendants of Judah) and are natively from the region land of Judea (land of the Jews). As revealed previously, the two regions known as Judea and Nazareth correspond to two conflicting lands. This revelation corresponds to the following description 'You are well aware that it is against our law for a Jew to associate with or visit a Gentile' – Acts 10:28.)

The next thing you must do is merge the revelations together into the correct context.

- {Nation of Esau} = {Ten Horns} = [Ten kings = Ten tribes: *(Ephraim, Manasseh, Naphtali, Dan, Asher, Issachar, Zebulon, Simeon, Reuben, and Gad)* = Nation of Ephraim = *who are yet to receive a kingdom of their own* = Kingdom of Samaria = Conquered by the Assyrian Empire = Exodus by the Kushite Empire *(Wadi of Egypt)*] = [2nd Exodus] = {Descendants of Esau} = {Eastern hill country} = {Land of Samaria} = {Land of the Gentiles} = [Region of Nazareth]

- {Nation of Jacob} = {Beast} = [single tribe: *(Benjamin)* = Nation of Judah = *remained in the city* = Conquered by Babylonian Empire = Exodus by the Persian Empire] = [2nd Exodus] = [Kingdom of Jerusalem] = {Descendants of Jacob} = {Western hill country} = {Land of Jerusalem} = {Land of the Jews} = [Hill region of Judea: *(Zechariah and Elizabeth)*] = [Region of Judea: *(Joseph - **Mary**)*]

{**Important note2:** Here, you must follow the Path of Joseph and Mary as they lead you through the western hill country, the land of Jerusalem}

THE PATH OF JOSEPH AND MARY

The next thing you must do is look closely at the bold portion in the following description of Luke 2:1-7 below,

[In those days Caesar Augustus issued a decree that a census should be taken of the entire Roman world. **And everyone went to his own town to register. So Joseph also went up from the town of Nazareth in Galilee to Judea, to Bethlehem the town of David,** because he belonged to the house and line of David]

Next, remove the following descriptions from the verses.

1- And everyone went to his own town to register
2- So Joseph also went up from the town of Nazareth in Galilee to Judea, to Bethlehem the town of David

(Note19: Within these two descriptions reveal a vital clue. For example: There is a hidden clue revealed in the following description 'went up from the town of Nazareth in Galilee to Judea, to Bethlehem the town of David.' To locate the hidden clue, you must start by dividing the following two regions to reflect their respective lands)

Look closely at the following descriptions as seen below,

- **{Region of Nazareth}** = [Eastern hill country] = [Land of the Gentiles] = [Land of Samaria]

- **{Region of Judea}** = [Western hill country] = [Land of the Jews] = [Land of Jerusalem]

*(Note20: If you look closely at the following revelations above you will notice the hidden clue is revealed behind this description '**Bethlehem the town of David.**' To reveal the clue that is hidden behind this description you must figure out which of the following two lands above correspond to the town of Jesse (David's father))*

Here is the next question. In what native land referring to the [(*eastern hill country*) and (*western hill country*)] does the town of Jesse natively correspond to?

(*Note21: The town of Jesse corresponds to a region within the eastern hill country, known as the town, called Bethlehem (also known as the town of Jesse the Ephrathite). This revelation corresponds to the following description – 'Now David was the son of an Ephrathite named Jesse, who was from Bethlehem in Judah' – 1Samuel 17:12. Bethlehem in Judah is symbolic and corresponds to the west bank region, the northeast region of the valley of Sychar. Thus, **Bethlehem** is symbolic and corresponds to a town in the eastern hill country, known as the town, called Sychar (the west bank region); and **in Judah** is symbolic and corresponds to the northeast region of the valley of Sychar*))

(*Note22: 'Bethlehem in Judah' is also symbolic and corresponds to the region known as Sokoh in Judah. This revelation also corresponds to the following description – 'Now the Philistines gathered their forces for war and assembled at Sokoh in Judah. They pitched camp at Ephes Dammim, between Sokoh and Azekah. Saul and the Israelites assembled and camped in the Valley of Elah and drew up their battle line to meet the Philistines. The Philistines occupied one hill and the Israelites another, with the valley between them' – 1ˢᵗ Samuel 17:1-3. For example: This part of the description **'Now the Philistines gathered their forces for war and assembled at Sokoh in Judah'** is symbolic and corresponds to the town called Sychar (as corresponding to 'Sokoh') and the northeast region of the valley of Sychar (as corresponding to 'in Judah'). This part of the description **'They pitched camp at Ephes Dammim,** is symbolic and corresponds to the northeast region of the valley of Sychar, the top terrain section of the valley. The top terrain section of the valley will be revealed in more detail in the later chapters. This part of the description **'between Sokoh and Azekah'** is also symbolic and corresponds to the northeast region of the valley of Sychar, the west bank and east bank regions. Thus, Sokoh is symbolic and corresponds to the town called Sychar (the west bank region), and Azekah is symbolic and corresponds to the city called Shechem (the east bank region)*))

(*Note23: Example2: This part of the description **'Saul and the Israelites assembled and camped in the Valley of Elah and drew up their battle line to meet the Philistines'** is also symbolic and corresponds to the southwest region of the valley of Sychar, the level terrain section of the valley. The level terrain section of the valley will be revealed in more detail in the later chapters. This revelation reveals the meaning behind the bold part of this description 'The Philistines occupied one hill and the Israelites another, __with the valley between them.__' Example3: This revelation also corresponds to this description **'Now a Levite*** *who lived in a remote area in the hill country of Ephraim* (southwest region of the Valley of Sychar) *took a concubine from Bethlehem in Judah* (northeast region of the Valley of Sychar)' – Judges 19:1. This revelation also corresponds to this description **'We are on our way from Bethlehem in Judah** (west bank region, the northeast region of the valley of Sychar) **to a remote area in the hill country of Ephraim where I live'** (the southwest region of the valley of Sychar). The southwest region of the valley also corresponds to the following description 'In another battle with the Philistines at Gob, Elhanan son of Jair the Bethlehemite killed the brother of Goliath the Gittite' – 2nd Samuel 21:19. Thus, the Valley of Elah is symbolic and corresponds to the Valley of Gob. This area represents the northeast entrance gate of Sychar that is located at the southwest region of the valley (also known as the level terrain section of the valley). The northeast entrance gate is also symbolic and corresponds to this description **'the gate of the town'** – 2 Samuel 18:4 (town called Sychar). The northeast entrance gate also corresponds to this description **'town gate of the city'** – Luke 7:12 (city called Shechem). The northeast entrance gate of Sychar also corresponds to the gate of Bethlehem. This revelation corresponds to the bold part of this description 'David longed for water and said, "Oh, that someone would get me a drink of water **from the well near the gate of Bethlehem!**" – 2 Samuel 23:15.' This revelation also corresponds to the bold description of the verse 'Now he had to go through Samaria. **So he came to a town in Samaria called Sychar,** (the northeast region of the valley of Sychar) **near the plot of ground Jacob had given to his son Joseph. Jacob's well was there** (southwest region of the valley of Sychar) – John 4:1-7. Therefore, the gate of Bethlehem, also called the gate of the town, is located near the well, called Jacob's Well. These revelations will be revealed in more detail in the 3rd Chronicle series titled The Elijah Doctrine3 (The Destination of the Sign))

Here is the next clue: **'Bethlehem the town of David,'** corresponds to **'Bethlehem in Judah'** *(the town of Jesse)* and correspond to the **'town called Sychar'** that is located at the northeast region of the valley of Sychar, the west bank region, and represents a region in the following land of the eastern hill country: [The land of Samaria]!

(Note24: Joseph (a native Jew) from the land of the western hill country, the land of Jerusalem, does not take Mary to **'Bethlehem the town of David'** *because the following region* **'Bethlehem in Judah'** *(the town of Jesse) corresponds to a region in the land of the eastern hill country, the land of Samaria. This revelation corresponds to the following description* **'For Jews do not associate with Samaritans'** *– John 4:9. The land of Samaria, also known as the land of Israel (land of the Gentiles) will be revealed in more detail as we move forward))*

Here is the next question. In what native region did everyone, including Joseph and Mary, go to register?

(Note25: According to the description of Luke 2:1 – 'Caesar Augustus issued a decree that a census should be taken of the entire Roman world.' However, the region that would have conducted the census pertaining to the land of the Jews reveals the next clue. For example: Joseph and Mary would not have had to travel a great distance to reach the central or capital region city within the land of Jerusalem to comply with Caesar's decree (this would have also applied to anyone living throughout the land of the Jews). Thus, this decree would have also applied to the eastern hill country land, in which the land of the Gentiles, would have had to journey to their own capital region city to comply with Caesar's written decree. The reason the two lands would have had to register in their own land can be revealed by these two verses: 'For Jews do not associate with Samaritans' – John 4:9 and 'You are well aware that it is against our law for a Jew to associate with or visit a Gentile' – Acts 10:28)

Here is the next clue: The native town *(went to their own town to register)* corresponds to a region of the western hill country land and represents the following capital region city that resides in the land of Jerusalem: [Jerusalem the Holy City]!

*(Note26: Jerusalem the Holy City represents the city where all native Jews must go to partake in the Passover Feast. This city represents the place where the Chief priest, High priest, and Levites, gather before the Temple courts (also known as Solomon's colonnade). This region is also where the Temple of the Lord is located as well as the marketplace. This revelation corresponds to the bold part of this description 'But other Jews were jealous; so they rounded up some bad characters from **the marketplace**, formed a mob and started a riot **in the city**' – Acts 17:5. This revelation also corresponds to the bold part of this description 'On reaching Jerusalem, Jesus **entered the temple courts and began driving out those who were buying and selling there. He overturned the tables of the money changers and the benches of those selling doves and would not allow anyone to carry merchandise through the temple courts**' – Mark 11:15-16. This city also represents the region where every male child must attend to undergo the ceremonial purification of circumcision in keeping with the Law of Moses as is the custom of the Jews))*

(Note27: Joseph does not take Mary to register in their native region (the region of Judea); nor does he take her to a region in the eastern hill country (the town of Jesse), but takes her to register in their capital region city within the western hill country, Jerusalem the Holy City))

The next thing you must do is merge the revelations together into the correct context.

- {Nation of Esau} = {Ten Horns} = [Ten kings = Ten tribes: *(Ephraim, Manasseh, Naphtali, Dan, Asher, Issachar, Zebulon, Simeon, Reuben, and Gad)* = Nation of Ephraim = *who are yet to receive a kingdom of their own* = Kingdom of Samaria = Conquered by the Assyrian Empire = Exodus by the Kushite Empire *(Wadi of Egypt)*] = [2nd Exodus] = {Descendants of Esau} = {Eastern hill country} = {Land of Samaria} = {Land of the Gentiles} = [Region of Nazareth]

- {Nation of Jacob} = {Beast} = [single tribe: *(Benjamin)* = Nation of Judah = *remained in the city* = Conquered by Babylonian Empire = Exodus by the Persian Empire] = [2nd Exodus] = [Kingdom of Jerusalem] = {Descendants of Jacob} = {Western hill country} = {Land of Jerusalem} = {Land of the Jews} = [Hill region of Judea: *(Zechariah and Elizabeth)*] = [Region of Judea: *(Joseph and Mary)*] = **[Capital region of Jerusalem = Jerusalem the Holy City]**

{**Important note3:** If you look closely at the description of the verses *'After Jesus was born in Bethlehem in Judea, during the time of King Herod, Magi from the east came to Jerusalem and asked, "Where is the one who has been born king of the Jews? We saw his star when it rose and have come to worship him." When King Herod heard this he was disturbed, and all Jerusalem with him'* – Matthew 2:1-3, you will soon discover it is a deceptive trap! For example: Within the verses lays two hidden clues. The 1st clue is revealed by the understanding of this description *'When King Herod heard this he was disturbed, and all Jerusalem with him.'* Thus, the King Herod you see in this description is not the King Herod you see. This revelation will be revealed in more detail moving forward. The 2nd clue is revealed by the understanding of this description *'After Jesus was born in Bethlehem in Judea.'* This revelation will be revealed in greater detail shortly}

THE BIRTHPLACE OF JESUS

The next thing you must do is look carefully at the bold portion in the following descriptions of Matthew 2:1-2 below,

[**After Jesus was born in Bethlehem in Judea**, during the time of King Herod, **Magi from the east came to Jerusalem** and asked, "Where is the one who has been born king of the Jews? **We saw his star in the east** and have come to worship him]

.

Next, remove the following descriptions from the verses.

1- After Jesus was born in Bethlehem in Judea
2- Magi from the east came to Jerusalem
3- We saw his star in the east

{**Important note4:** These descriptions also reveal another vital clue. The clue is revealed behind the revelation of the Magi. To uncover the clue, you must follow the Magi as they travel away from the land of the east, the eastern hill country, the land of Samaria, and towards the land of the west, the western hill country, the land of Jerusalem}

The first thing you must do is re-list the following description below,

- [Magi from the east came to Jerusalem]

(Note29: The land of the east (where the Magi traveled away from) corresponds to the eastern hill country, the land of the Gentiles. Thus, the Magi traveled away from the land of the eastern hill country, the land of Samaria, and have set out for the land of the western hill country, the Land of Jerusalem, the land of the Jews))

Next, re-list the following description below,

- [We saw his star in the east]

(Note30: This description is written deceptively and reveals a hidden clue. For example: The star in the east does not represent a star seen in the night sky as being viewed from the east. The star in this description corresponds to the Sun, also known as sunrise (thus, the Sun appears to rise in the land of the east during the summer solstice and will set to the land of the west). The clue, however, is concealed within Matthew 2:9)

Look closely at the bold portion in the following description of Matthew 2:9 below,

[After they had heard the king, they went on their way, and **the star they had seen in the east went ahead of them** until it stopped over the place where the child was]

(Note31: If the star (Sun) seen in the east as representing (sunrise) went ahead of them, then the direction in which the Sun travels is west toward sunset. Therefore, during the summer solstice the Sun cannot be seen from the east if traveling in the western direction (for the Magi would have seen the Sun move ahead of them). Thus, the Sun would be seen in the west (went ahead of them from the east). The next clue is revealed by the understanding as to where in the land of the west does the Sun appear to stop! To locate the next clue, you must re-list the next description removed from the verses)

Next, re-list the following description removed from the verses.

- [After Jesus was born in Bethlehem in Judea]

*(Note32: This description is also written deceptively and reveals a hidden clue: For example: The following description 'Bethlehem in Judea' does not represent a region in the land of the western hill country. There are three regions that collectively make up the land of the western hill country, the land of Jerusalem. These regions are as follows: **Bethany**, **Jerusalem the Holy City,** and **Judea**. This revelation will be revealed in more detail moving forward. This description* **'Bethlehem in Judea'** *is symbolic and reveals a paradox to this description* **'to Bethlehem the town of David'** *– Luke 2:7. For example: <u>Bethlehem in Judea</u> corresponds to <u>Bethlehem the town of David</u>. However, both descriptions are symbolic and correspond to the region known as 'Bethlehem in Judah (the town of Jesse).' As revealed previously, 'Bethlehem in Judah' corresponds to the west bank region, the northeast region of the valley of Sychar, the town called Sychar. This revelation corresponds to the following description 'he came to a town in Samaria called Sychar – John 4:5. Thus, 'Bethlehem in Judea' (the so-called town of David) is the same as saying 'Bethlehem in Judah' (the so-called town of Jesse). Therefore, both descriptions refer to the west bank region, the northeast region of the Valley of Sychar))*

(Note33: Could Jesus have been born in the region land of the eastern hill country (the northeast region of the valley of Sychar)? Or could he have been born in a land foreign to both the western hill country, the land of Jerusalem; and the eastern hill country, the land of Samaria? To locate the next clue, you must look closely at the bold portion in the following description of Matthew 2:9)

Look closely at the bold portion in the following description of Matthew 2:9 below,

[After they had heard the king, they went on their way, and the star they had seen in the east went ahead of them **until it stopped over the place where the child was**]

(Note34: According to the account, when the Magi appeared before King Herod, they were instructed to return upon their finding concerning the place where the child was to be born. This revelation corresponds to the following description 'And sending them to Bethlehem, he said: "Go, search carefully for the Child, and when you find Him, report to me, so that I too may go and worship Him" – Matthew 2:7. The verse of Matthew 2:7, is written deceptively for three important reasons. Reason One: Judea represents a region of

28

the western hill country, the land of Jerusalem. However, Judea does not represent the name of the western hill country, nor is Judea the name of a country. Therefore, no king was installed to rule over only a particular region of the western hill country (referring to the region of Judea). Reason Two: The land of Jerusalem was not presided over by a King. Thus, King Herod never ruled over the land of Jerusalem, nor did he preside as Lord over the land of the Jews, the western hill country, in the time of Zechariah, Elizabeth, Joseph and Mary, nor at any other time. This revelation will be revealed in more detail following the path of John, the son of Zechariah. On the contrary, King Herod represents the king of the eastern hill country, the land of Samaria (thus, he presides as Lord over the land of the Gentiles). This revelation corresponds to the following description 'When he learned that Jesus was under King Herod's jurisdiction, he sent him to Herod' – Luke 23:7. Therefore, the person of authority the Magi would have appeared before would have been, none other than, Abijah the Chief priest! Abijah the Chief priest, reigns over the priestly division in the time of Zechariah, Elizabeth, Joseph and Mary (thus, he presides as Lord over the land of Jerusalem). This revelation corresponds to the description 'Then the chief priests, the teachers of the law and the elders looked for a way to arrest him' – Mark 12:12. This revelation also corresponds to the following description 'Why didn't you arrest me in the Temple? I was there among you teaching every day' - Mark 14:49. This revelation reveals the meaning behind the bold description of the verse, '"What charges are you bringing against this man?" "If he were not a criminal," they replied, "we would not have handed him over to you." Pilate said, "Take him yourselves and judge him by your own law." – John 18:29-31. With that said, the Magi would not have left the palace of King Herod (the eastern hill country, the land of Samaria); but would have left the Temple court (the western hill country, the land of Jerusalem). Therefore, the Magi would have met with Abijah in the capital region of the western hill country, before continuing their journey, traveling in the western direction from Jerusalem the Holy City (would not have set out from the region of Judea). This revelation is revealed by the following description 'After they had heard the king (Abijah the Chief priest), they went on their way (leaving the Temple court)' – Matthew 2:9. This revelation reveals the direction, in which the star, the Magi seen in the east (the land of King Herod), went ahead of them traveling west toward the land of Jerusalem (the land of Abijah, the Chief priest). Reason Three: The next region land (traveling west outside the region capital city, Jerusalem the Holy City) is the region called Bethany; not Bethlehem in Judea! This revelation corresponds to the following description 'Now Bethany was less than two miles from Jerusalem' – John 11:18 (Jerusalem being symbolic for representing Jerusalem, the Holy City). Thus, the Sun only sets towards the region land of Bethany during the summer solstice (does not however appear to stop in the region land of Bethany, during the changing of the solstice))

(Note35: The following description **'the exact time the star had appeared'** – Matthew 2:7, is symbolic and corresponds to a particular day in the land of the west (surpassing the region of Bethany) where the summer solstice will draw near to its end. This phenomenon is known as an astronomical event that takes place in the land of the west once every year (Thus, the words 'the exact time' corresponds to the exact day and moment). This revelation corresponds to the bold part of this description '**until it stopped** over the place where the child was.' This event represents the changing of the solstice and is known as the event that marks the end of the summer solstice. Thus, on December 21st the Sun will stop, reverse, rise again, and the winter solstice will begin in the northern hemisphere. It is during this moment when the Sun (traveling west towards nightfall) will appear to stop along the equator (in the tropic of Capricorn). When the changing of the solstice is complete, the Sun will appear to rise again, and set in the opposite direction of sunrise. This revelation reveals the meaning behind this description **"We saw his star when it rose."** – Matthew 2:2.))

(Note36: The following description 'we saw his star in the east' is a deceptive trap! This is due to the perceived behavior of the Sun during the summer solstice, in which the Sun appears to rise in the land of the east as representing sunrise and set to the land of the west as representing sunset. The star (also known as the Sun) was seen by the Magi in the land of the west, known as the Kushite land of Egypt (the exact time the star had appeared). This revelation is revealed by the following description '**After they had heard the king** (Abijah the Chief priest) **they went on their way** (traveling west of the city) **and the star they had seen in the east** (from sunrise) **went ahead of them** (towards sunset). Therefore, the Magi continued west, less than two miles, outside of Jerusalem the Holy City, then passed the region land of Bethany, and entered the land of Egypt (the land where the Sun will appear to stop))

(Note37: The 'star' (Sun) according to the description 'the exact time the star had appeared' does not represent a celestial star viewed in the night sky. Thus, the changing of the solstice does not occur in the evening of the day as representing nightfall. On the contrary, the changing of the solstice occurs in the daylight hours as representing the afternoon. Therefore, this description '**the exact time the star had appeared'** means the Magi would have seen the Sun (beginning of the solstice change) in the afternoon hours of the day (as representing daylight) and not the evening of day (as representing nightfall). This revelation corresponds to this description '**until it stopped!'** This revelation reveals the meaning behind this description '**When they saw the star, they were overjoyed'** – Matthew 2:10. December 21st marks the day in which the solstice will begin its change, by coming to a halt (until it stopped) before it begins its *reverse. When the changing of the solstice is complete the Sun will appear to rise again (**We saw his star when it rose**) and set in the opposite direction of sunrise towards the land of the east))*

Here is the final clue: Jesus was born in the following land of the west: [The Wadi of Egypt]!

To illustrate this, merge the revelations together into the correct context regarding the Summer Solstice.

- **{Sunrises from the land of the east}** = {Descendants of Esau} **=** {Eastern hill country} = {Land of Samaria} = {Land of the Gentiles} = [District region of Nazareth]

- **{Sunsets towards the land of the west}** = {Descendants of Jacob} = {Western hill country} = {Land of Jerusalem} = {Land of the Jews} = [Hill region of Judea: *(Zechariah and Elizabeth)*] = [Region of Judea: *(Joseph and Mary)*] = [Region Capital: Jerusalem the Holy City] = **[Region of Bethany *(less than two miles from Jerusalem, the Holy City)*]**

- **{Sun stops in the land of the west *(solstice change in the afternoon)*}** = {Land of the west} = [Kingdom of Cush (Wadi of Egypt)] = [Western region of Egypt = Punt (Libyans)] = [Eastern region of Egypt = Put (Nubians) = The Red Sea] = **[Land of Egypt: *(birthplace of Jesus)*]**

The next thing you must do is look closely at the bold portion in the following description of Matthew 2:15 below,

[where he stayed until the death of Herod. **And so was fulfilled what the Lord had said through the prophet: "Out of Egypt I called my son."**]

*(Note38: This description reveals another vital clue. For example: The birth of Jesus is symbolic and corresponds to the birth of a sign (not revealed in the 1ˢᵗ Chronicle, titled the Elijah Doctrine, Revelation of the Sign). This revelation will reveal the meaning behind the bold portion of this description 'She was pregnant and cried out in pain as she was about to give birth. **Then another sign appeared in heaven'** – Revelation 12:2-3.)*

To reveal the next clue, you must bring back the base decoder revealed in the 1st Chronicle of the Elijah Doctrine (Revelation of the Sign) and look closely at the bold portion regarding the revelations revealed by Dinah *(as representing the waters you saw where the prostitute sits, the Queen of the South, and a woman clothed with the sun))*

Look closely at the bold portion in the following revelation below,

- [5th prominent horn] = [Solid gold lampstand = Someone like a son of man = Michael = Man clothed in linen (writing kit at his side) = *He came and took the scroll from the right hand of him who sat on the throne! = The armies of heaven were following him, riding.on white horses and dressed in fine linen, white and clean = (And from His mouth proceeds a sharp sword) =* 8th king = King of Kings = Lord of Lords = Naphtali] = [5th beast = Woman = Dinah = 5th living creature = Lamb looking as though slain *(will hate the prostitute)* = 5th cherubim = 5th chariot = White horses = 5th angel = 5th guard of the city = 5th apocalyptic rider *(from His mouth proceeds a sharp sword)* = White horses = A great hailstorm] = **[twelfth tribe = The tribe of Dinah = *started small but grew in power* = 5th kingdom = Element of Rock = Coming Age]** = **{Pharaoh Tirhakah *(Pharoah of Egypt)*} = [Empire of Kush] = [Land divided by rivers: *(Blue Nile River)* and *(White Nile River)*] = [a people tall and smooth-skinned, to a people feared far and wide, an aggressive nation of strange speech] = [Invaded the land of Egypt *(Egypt fell in the 25th dynasty)*] = [Invaded the land of Assyria (captured the Samarian Israelites)] = [Ancient Nubia *(land of the Kushites)*] = [Western region of upper Egypt = Punt *(Libyans)*] and [Eastern region of upper Egypt = Put *(Nubians)* = The Red Sea *(waters you saw where the prostitute sits)*] = [Queen of the South *(Woman clothed with the sun)* = A great and wondrous sign = 5th spirit = The Sun = The passing of the Sign of Jonah *(summer solstice ends in the southern hemisphere)* = End of the Summer Solstice *(on Dec 21st)*]**

(Note39: Dinah, (as corresponding to the Queen of the South) who journeys from the north to the land of the south (the Wadi of Egypt) is also symbolic and corresponds to Mary, the mother who travels from the east to the land of the west (the land of Egypt))

*(Note40: The **'birth of Immanuel,'** born to Dinah (born in the land of the **south**) is symbolic and corresponds to the birth of the next great sign that would appear over the waters of the Red Sea, in the Wadi of Egypt. This revelation will correspond to the following description "The virgin will conceive and give birth to a son, and they will call him Immanuel" - Matthew 1:23 (the virgin as corresponding to the virgin daughter of Jacob, who was raped))*

*(Note41: The **'birth of Jesus,'** born to Mary (born in the land of the **west**) is also symbolic and corresponds to the birth of the next great sign that would appear over the waters of the Red Sea, in the land of Egypt. This revelation will correspond to the following description 'Behold, you will conceive and give birth to a son, and you shall give him the name Jesus. He will be great and will be called the Son of the Most High' – Luke 1:31-32)*

*(Note42: The following two directions corresponding to both births (**south** and **west**) are also symbolic and correspond to the Kushite land of Egypt. Thus, the directions, south and west, correspond to the tropic of Capricorn. For example: south and west represents the coordinates '**south** of true **west**' and corresponds to the solstice change (the passing of the Sign of Jonah), in which the Sun will stop in the tropic of Capricorn, south of true west (marking the end of the summer solstice). This revelation reveals the meaning behind these descriptions '**the exact time the star had appeared**' (December 21st, as marking the day, in which the summer solstice ends in the southern hemisphere) and '**until it stopped over the place where the child was**' (the solstice changes and reverses). South of true west also corresponds to the start of the winter solstice, in which the Sun will rise again (reverse in the tropic of Capricorn) from the same coordinates (south of true west). The completion of the solstice change fulfills the meaning behind this description '**We saw his star when it rose**' (winter begins in the northern hemisphere))*

Here is the final revelation: The birth of Immanuel *(born in the land of the south)* and the birth of Jesus *(born in the land of the west)* corresponds to the start of the winter solstice *(born south of true west)* and represents the birth of the following sign: [The Sign of Ezekiel].

*(Note43: The sign of Ezekiel corresponds to the bold portion of this description '<u>**Ezekiel will be a sign to you**</u>; according to all that he has done you will do; <u>**when it comes, then you will know**</u> that I am the Lord God' - Ezekiel 24:24. The Sign of Ezekiel fulfills the meaning behind this description '**Then another sign appeared in heaven**' – Revelation 12:2-3. The passing of the Sign of Ezekiel as well as the birth of the sign of Jonah will also be revealed in more detail at the conclusion of this book)*

The final thing you must do is merge the revelations together into the correct context.

- {[Dinah *(give birth in the land of the south)* = **Mary *(give birth in the land of the west)***]} = [Queen of the South *(Sun sets to the land of the south)* = **Mother of the west *(Sun sets to the land of the west)***] = [Wadi of Egypt *(Sun stops in the tropic of Capricorn - **south of true west**)* = The passing of the Sign of Jonah ***(summer solstice ends in the southern hemisphere on December 21ˢᵗ)***]

- {[Immanuel *(born in the land of the south)* = **Jesus *(born in the land of the west)***]} = [Born sons *(Sun rises in the land of the south)* and ***(Sun rises in the land of the west)***] = [Kushite land of Egypt ***(Solstice reverses in the tropic of Capricorn - south of true west)*** = **The birth of the Sign of Ezekiel *(winter solstice is born in the northern hemisphere on December 21ˢᵗ)***}

*(Note44: The **end of the summer solstice** which ends in the southern hemisphere (the exact time the star had appeared), fulfills the meaning behind this description '**But in the days when the seventh angel is about to sound his trumpet**' – **Revelation 10:7**. For example: The sound of the trumpet blast as representing the sound of '**shouts**' corresponds to Dinah (gives birth in the land of the south) and Mary (gives birth in the land of the west). This revelation corresponds to this description '**until it stopped**'! Thus, revealing December 21ˢᵗ as the day, the two will deliver (summer solstice ends in the southern hemisphere, in the land of Egypt, south of true west))*

*(Note45: The **start of the winter solstice** (We saw his star when it rose), fulfills the meaning behind this description '**the mystery of God will be accomplished, just as he announced to his servants the prophets**' – **Revelation 10:7**. For example: Immanuel is born in the land of the south and Jesus is born in the land of the west. Thus, also revealing December 21ˢᵗ as the day of their birth (winter solstice is born in the northern hemisphere, in the land of Egypt, south of true west). This revelation reveals the meaning behind this description '**when it comes, then you will know that I am the Lord God**' - Ezekiel 24:24.)*

{**Important note4:** If you look closely at this description *'Today in the town of David a Savior has been born to you; he is the Messiah, the Lord'* – Luke 2:11, you will discover it is a deceptive trap! For example: As the revelations has proven, Jesus was not born in the land of the western hill country, the land of Jerusalem. Example2: As previously revealed, the town of David *(Bethlehem in Judea)* corresponds to the town of Jesse *(Bethlehem in Judah)* and represents a town in the land of the eastern hill country, in the land of Samaria, known as the town called Sychar *(west bank region, the northeast region of the valley of Sychar)*}

{**Important note5:** Jesus is symbolic and represents the Sun, and his birth, is also symbolic and represents the start of the winter solstice, born in the land of Egypt *(south of true west in the tropic of Capricorn)*}

Congratulations! You have successfully revealed the 1st woe hidden behind the 1st miraculous sign:

….. Jesus was not born in the land of the eastern hill country, the land of Samaria; nor was he born in the land of the western hill country, the land of Jerusalem. He was born in the land of the west, the Kushite land of Nubia, the Wadi of Egypt …..

CHAPTER TWO- 2ND PHASE OF THE CRYPTEX PUZZLE- THE PATH OF THE SIGN

The second test in this Chapter is to unveil the mystery revealed behind the [2nd woe] by revealing the revelation concealed behind the 2nd miraculous sign: [**Jesus baptized in the Jordan River**]!

(Note: To solve this mystery you must follow the child born in the Kushite land of Egypt as he journeys from the land of the west and towards the land of the eastern hill country)

The first thing you must do is look closely at the bold portion in the following description of Matthew 2:19-23 below,

[After Herod died, an angel of the Lord appeared in a dream to Joseph in Egypt and said, "Get up, **take the child and his mother and go to the land of Israel,** for those who were trying to take the child's life are dead. So he got up, took the child and his mother and **went to the land of Israel.** But when he heard that Archelaus was reigning **in Judea** in place of his father Herod, **he was afraid to go there.** Having been warned in a dream, **he withdrew to the district of Galilee, and he went and lived in a town called Nazareth.** So was fulfilled what was said through the prophets: **"He will be called a Nazarene]**

Next, remove the bold descriptions from the verses.

> 1- take the child and his mother and go to the land of Israel
> 2- went to the land of Israel
> 3- in Judea
> 4- he was afraid to go there
> 5- he withdrew to the district of Galilee, and he went and lived in a town called Nazareth.
> 6- "He will be called a Nazarene"

Next, re-list the following description removed from the verses below,

- [take the child and his mother and go to the land of Israel]

(Note2: This description reveals a major clue. For example: The land of Israel is symbolic and corresponds to the land of the eastern hill country, also known as the land of the Gentiles (the descendant land of Ephraim))

(Note3: The land of Israel does not correspond to the land of the western hill country, the land of Jerusalem, also known as the land of the Jews (the descendants of Judah))

Here is the next clue: The land of Israel corresponds to the following land of the eastern hill country *(land of the Gentiles)* and represents the following land: [The land of Samaria *(descendants of Esau)*].

37

The next thing you must do is merge the revelations together into the correct context.

- {Nation of Esau} = {Ten Horns} = [Ten kings = Ten tribes: *(Ephraim, Manasseh, Naphtali, Dan, Asher, Issachar, Zebulon, Simeon, Reuben, and Gad)* = Nation of Ephraim = *who are yet to receive a kingdom of their own* = Kingdom of Samaria = Conquered by the Assyrian Empire = Exodus by the Kushite Empire *(Wadi of Egypt)*] = [2nd Exodus] = {Descendants of Esau} = {Eastern hill country} = {Land of Samaria} = **{Land of Israel}** = {Land of the Gentiles} = [District region of Nazareth]

- {Nation of Jacob} = {Beast} = [single tribe: *(Benjamin)* = Nation of Judah = *remained in the city* = Conquered by Babylonian Empire = Exodus by the Persian Empire] = [2nd Exodus] = [Kingdom of Jerusalem] = {Descendants of Jacob} = {Western hill country} = {Land of Jerusalem} = {Land of the Jews} = [Hill region of Judea: *(Zechariah and Elizabeth)*] = [Region of Judea: *(Joseph and Mary)*] = [Capital region of Jerusalem = Jerusalem the Holy City] = [Region of Bethany *(less than two miles from Jerusalem the Holy City)*]

Next, re-list the following description removed from the verses.

- [in Judea, he was afraid to go there]

(Note4: This description reveals another major clue. For example: There are two reasons Joseph was afraid to return to his native region (the region of Judea). The first is as follow: The birth of Jesus (though symbolic) constitutes Mary having conceived a child out of wedlock (thus, breaking the Law of Moses). The second is as follows: Joseph and Mary never registered in their native land according to Cesar's decree that a censes be taken of the entire Roman world (thus, having no share in the covenant of the Jews). To reveal the clue, you must look closely at the next description removed from the verses))

Look closely at the following description below,

- [he withdrew to the district of Galilee, and he went and lived in a town called Nazareth]

(Note5: This description also reveals a hidden clue. For example: As previously revealed, the region of Nazareth (region in the land of the Gentiles) borders the region known as the hill region of Judea (land of the Jews). However, the hidden clue is that Nazareth represents one of the four districts of Galilee that make up the land of the eastern hill country, the land of Samaria))

Here is the next clue: The 'town called Nazareth' corresponds to the 'region called Nazareth' and represents the following district of Galilee: [1st district of Galilee].

The next thing you must do is merge the revelations together into the correct context.

- {Nation of Esau} = {Ten Horns} = [Ten kings = Ten tribes: *(Ephraim, Manasseh, Naphtali, Dan, Asher, Issachar, Zebulon, Simeon, Reuben, and Gad)* **=** Nation of Ephraim = *who are yet to receive a kingdom of their own* = Kingdom of Samaria = Conquered by the Assyrian Empire = Exodus by the Kushite Empire *(Wadi of Egypt)*] = [2nd Exodus] = {Descendants of Esau} **=** {Eastern hill country} = {Land of Samaria} = {Land of Israel} = {Land of the Gentiles} = [**1st District of Galilee** = District region of Nazareth]

- {Nation of Jacob} = {Beast} = [single tribe: *(Benjamin)* **=** Nation of Judah = *remained in the city* = Conquered by Babylonian Empire = Exodus by the Persian Empire] = [2nd Exodus] = [Kingdom of Jerusalem] = {Descendants of Jacob} = {Western hill country} = {Land of Jerusalem} = {Land of the Jews} = [Hill region of Judea: *(Zechariah and Elizabeth)*] = [Region of Judea: *(Joseph and Mary)*] = [Capital region of Jerusalem = Jerusalem the Holy City] = [Region of Bethany *(less than two miles from Jerusalem the Holy City)*]

Next, re-list the following description removed from the verses.

- ["He will be called a Nazarene"]

(Note6: This description reveals another major clue. For example: Joseph and Mary go to live in the land of Israel (land of the Gentiles) because he was afraid to return to his native region of the western hill country))

Here is the next clue: Joseph and Mary go into exile away from their native land, the land of the western hill country, the land of Jerusalem, to live in the following land of the eastern hill country: [The Land of Samaria]

*(Note7: Jesus does not belong to the house and line of David because he was born in the Kushite land of Egypt (will not share in the covenant of the Jews). Thus, he will not be called a Jew; but will be called a Nazarene, a Galilean, a Samaritan, and a Gentile. This revelation corresponds to the following description 'On hearing this, **Pilate asked if the man was a <u>Galilean</u>**. When he learned that Jesus was under Herod's jurisdiction, he sent him to Herod' – Luke 23:6-7)*

Here is the next question. Was Jesus circumcised according to the custom of the Jews *(in keeping with the Law of Moses)* or did he remain uncircumcised according to the custom of the Gentiles?

(Note8: This question reveals another vital clue. For example: The practice of circumcision represents the practice, known as the purification of circumcision. The answer to this question will be revealed behind the hidden clue found in the description of Luke 2:21-22)

THE PURIFICATION OF CIRCUMCISION

Look closely at the bold portion in the following descriptions of Luke 2:21-22 below,

[On the eighth day, when it was time to circumcise him, he was named Jesus, the name the angel had given him before he had been conceived. **When the time of their purification according to the Law of Moses had been completed, Joseph and Mary took him to Jerusalem to present him to the Lord]**

Next, remove the following descriptions from the verses.

1- On the eighth day, when it was time to circumcise him
2- When the time of their purification according to the Law of Moses had been completed
3- Joseph and Mary took him to Jerusalem to present him to the Lord

*(Note9: The **'eighth day'** reveals the hidden clue. For example: The eighth day represents the day when every male child (descendants of Judah) living in the land of the Jews (western hill country) must be circumcised according to the custom of the Jews (descendants of Jacob). This custom is known as the purification of circumcision. This revelation corresponds to the following description 'On the eighth day the boy is to be circumcised' – Leviticus 12:3)*

Here is the next clue: Jesus was not circumcised on the eighth day according to the custom of the Jews!

(Note10: Joseph and Mary (afraid to return to Judea) are now considered exiled from their native land (land of Jerusalem). This revelation corresponds to the description 'he will be called a Nazarene (will live in the custom of the Gentiles, not in the custom of the Jews))

(Note11: Joseph and Mary remained in exile to the land of the eastern hill country and does not take Jesus to their native land (the western hill country) to present him before the temple courts in the Capital Region City, known as Jerusalem the Holy City. This revelation also corresponds to the following description 'You are well aware that it is against our law for a Jew to associate with or visit a Gentile' – Acts 10:28.)

The next thing you must do is look closely at the bold portion in the descriptions below,

Luke 2:39 – [**When Joseph and Mary had done everything required by the Law of the Lord, they returned to Galilee to their own town of Nazareth**]

Luke 2:41-43 – [**Every year his parents went to Jerusalem for the Feast of the Passover. When he was twelve years old, they went up to the Feast, according to the custom.** After the Feast was over, while his parents were returning home, **the boy Jesus stayed behind in Jerusalem**, but they were unaware of it]

Next, remove the following descriptions from the verses.

1- When Joseph and Mary had done everything required by the Law of the Lord, they returned to Galilee to their own town of Nazareth
2- Every year his parents went to Jerusalem for the Feast of the Passover. When he was twelve years old, they went up to the Feast, according to the custom.
3- the boy Jesus stayed behind in Jerusalem

(Note12: The first description above is misleading! For example: The land of Jerusalem (descendants of Judah); and the land of Samaria (descendant land of Ephraim), represents two conflicting lands (thus, 'Ephraim broke away from Judah' – Isaiah 7:17). Therefore, the land of the Jews due not associate with the land of the Gentiles. Thus, if any native from the land of Jerusalem (the western hill country) goes into exile to the land of Samaria, the eastern hill country, that person or persons must remain in exile to that land and would never be able to return (will be considered a Gentile, a Samaritan, and a Galilean). Though, Jesus would be called a Nazarene, (from the region of Nazareth) he would also be called a Gentile, a Samaritan, and a Galilean)

*(Note13: The second and third descriptions above reveal a very important revelation and contains a vital clue. For example: The parents in this description **'Every year his parents went to Jerusalem for the Feast of the Passover'** does not represent Joseph and Mary but corresponds to the parents of someone else. This revelation will be revealed in detail moving forward. Example2: The boy in this description **'the boy Jesus stayed behind in Jerusalem'** does not represent Jesus but corresponds to the child of someone else. This revelation will also be revealed in detail moving forward)*

The next thing you must do is merge the revelations together into the correct context.

- {Nation of Esau} = {Ten Horns} = [Ten kings = Ten tribes: *(Ephraim, Manasseh, Naphtali, Dan, Asher, Issachar, Zebulon, Simeon, Reuben, and Gad)* = Nation of Ephraim = *who are yet to receive a kingdom of their own* = Kingdom of Samaria = Conquered by the Assyrian Empire = Exodus by the Kushite Empire *(Wadi of Egypt)*] = [2nd Exodus] = {Descendants of Esau} = {Eastern hill country} = {Land of Samaria} = {Land of Israel} = {Land of the Gentiles} = [1st District of Galilee = District region of Nazareth ***(Joseph, Mary and Jesus exiled)***]

- {Nation of Jacob} = {Beast} = [single tribe: *(Benjamin)* = Nation of Judah = *remained in the city* = Conquered by Babylonian Empire = Exodus by the Persian Empire] = [2nd Exodus] = [Kingdom of Jerusalem] = {Western hill country} = {Descendants of Jacob} = {Land of Jerusalem} = {Land of the Jews} = [Hill region of Judea: *(Zechariah and Elizabeth)*] = [Region of Judea: *(Joseph and Mary)*] = [Capital region of Jerusalem = Jerusalem the Holy City] = [Region of Bethany *(less than two miles from Jerusalem the Holy City)*]

{**Important note:** Here is where the path of Joseph and Mary will end *(continued to live in exile to the land of the eastern hill country, the 1st district of Galilee, the region called Nazareth)*. Here, you must now follow the path of Jesus as he journeys outside the 1st district of Galilee, the region of Nazareth}

The first thing you must do is look closely at the bold portion in the following description of Matthew 4:13-16.

[Leaving Nazareth, he went and lived in Capernaum, which was **by the lake in the area of Zebulun and Naphtali**- to fulfill what was said through the prophet Isaiah: "**Land of Zebulun and land of Naphtali, the way to the sea, along the Jordan, Galilee of the Gentiles**- the people living in darkness have seen a great light; on those living in the land of the shadow of death a light has dawned]

Next, remove the following descriptions from the verses.

1- Leaving Nazareth, he went and lived in Capernaum
2- by the lake in the area of Zebulun and Naphtali
3- Land of Zebulun and land of Naphtali, the way to the sea, along the Jordan, Galilee of the Gentiles

(Note14: These descriptions above reveal another major clue: For example: The land of Zebulun and land of Naphtali corresponds to the region, called Capernaum (thus, Capernaum consist of two region lands that are divided by a body of water). The body of water that divides the two lands does not represent a lake but is known as the Jordan River. The hidden clue is that the region of Capernaum, also represents one of the districts of Galilee, in the land of Samaria))

Here is the next clue: The land of Zebulun and land of Naphtali corresponds to the region called Capernaum *(along the Jordan)* and represents the following district of Galilee: [2nd district of Galilee].

The next thing you must do is merge the revelations together into the correct context.

- {Nation of Esau} = {Ten Horns} = [Ten kings = Ten tribes: *(Ephraim, Manasseh, Naphtali, Dan, Asher, Issachar, Zebulon, Simeon, Reuben, and Gad)* = Nation of Ephraim = *who are yet to receive a kingdom of their own* = Kingdom of Samaria = Conquered by the Assyrian Empire = Exodus by the Kushite Empire *(Wadi of Egypt)*] = [2nd Exodus] = {Descendants of Esau} = {Eastern hill country} = {Land of Samaria} = {Land of Israel} = {Land of the Gentiles} = [1st District of Galilee = District region of Nazareth *(Joseph, Mary and Jesus exiled)*] = **[2nd District of Galilee = District region of Capernaum *(Land of Zebulun and land of Naphtali, the way to the sea, along the Jordan)*]**

- {Nation of Jacob} = {Beast} = [single tribe: *(Benjamin)* = Nation of Judah = *remained in the city* = Conquered by Babylonian Empire = Exodus by the Persian Empire] = [2nd Exodus] = [Kingdom of Jerusalem] = {Descendants of Jacob} = {Western hill country} = {Land of Jerusalem} = {Land of the Jews} = [Hill region of Judea: *(Zechariah and Elizabeth)*] = [Region of Judea: *(Joseph and Mary)*] = [Capital region of Jerusalem = Jerusalem the Holy City] = [Region of Bethany *(less than two miles from Jerusalem the Holy City)*]

The next thing you must do is re-list the entire descriptions removed from the verses and place the bold descriptions in the correct number order according to the context of the story.

[1] **Leaving Nazareth, he went** and lived [2] **in Capernaum**
by the lake in the area of Zebulun and Naphtali
[3] **Land of Zebulun and land of Naphtali, the way to the sea, along the Jordan,**
Galilee of the Gentiles

Next, remove the bold descriptions in numbered order and reconstruct them into the correct context of the story as seen below,

[1] Leaving Nazareth, he went [2] in Capernaum [3] Land of Zebulun and land of Naphtali, the way to the sea, along the Jordan

To reveal the first piece to the sacred document of Immanuel you must merge the revelations into the correct context as seen below,

[Leaving Nazareth *(1ˢᵗ district of Galilee)*, he went in Capernaum *(2ⁿᵈ district of Galilee)* Land of Zebulun and land of Naphtali, the way to the sea *(Sea of Galilee)*, along the Jordan *(Jordan River)*]

(Note15: When Jesus leaves the 1ˢᵗ district of Galilee (the region of Nazareth) he enters the 2ⁿᵈ district of Galilee (the region of Capernaum). However, the following description 'Leaving Nazareth, he went and lived in Capernaum' reveals another hidden clue. For example: Did Jesus live in Capernaum after leaving Nazareth or is he merely passing through the 2ⁿᵈ district of Galilee? The answer to this question will be revealed in detail shortly!)

The next thing you must do is look carefully at the bold portion in the following description of John 1:43-45 below,

[The next day Jesus decided to leave for Galilee. Finding Philip, he said to him, "Follow me."
Philip, like Andrew and Peter, was from the town of Bethsaida]

Next, remove the following descriptions from the verses.

1- The next day Jesus decided to leave for Galilee
2- Philip, like Andrew and Peter, was from the town of Bethsaida

*(Note16: There are three major clues revealed within these descriptions. For example: If you look closely at the following description 'The next day Jesus decided to leave for Galilee' you would discover the answer to the previous question regarding if Jesus lived in Capernaum or merely passes through the 2nd district of Galilee. One of the clues is revealed by the bold part of this description (**the way to the sea**, along the Jordan River). The other clue is revealed by the bold part of this description: '**The next day** Jesus decided to leave.' For example: This description 'The next day' is symbolic and reveals the region of Capernaum to be approximately within a one day's journey by foot through the entire district. This description 'the way to the sea' reveals the border of the 2nd district of Galilee (along the Jordan River). Thus, the Sea of Galilee reveals you are no longer in the 2nd district of Galilee. Therefore, the region called Capernaum ends at the Jordan River))*

*(Note17: The final clue is revealed behind the understanding of this description: '**decided to leave for Galilee**.' This revelation is revealed behind the understanding of which district of Galilee does Jesus decide to leave for? For example: The 'district of Galilee' (Jesus decided to leave for), corresponds to the native region of Philip, Nathanael, Andrew, and Simon, known as the region of Bethsaida (the way to the Sea). Thus, the town of Bethsaida is symbolic and corresponds to the region called Bethsaida. This region of Galilee represents the next district region of Galilee that resides outside of the 2nd district of Galilee. Therefore, the answer to the previous question is, Jesus passes through the 2nd district of Galilee)*

*(Note18: Jesus does not leave his native region of Nazareth, known as the 1ˢᵗ district of Galilee, to live in the 2ⁿᵈ district of Galilee, known as the region of Capernaum. On the contrary, he merely passes through the region of Capernaum (**along the Jordan River**) to reach the region of Bethsaida (**the way to the sea**). The body of water in the region of Bethsaida is called the Sea of Galilee. Therefore, the region of Bethsaida also represents a district of Galilee, in the land of Samaria)*

Here is the next clue: The following description **'The next day Jesus decided to leave for Galilee'** corresponds to the region called Bethsaida and represents the following district region of Galilee: [3ʳᵈ District of Galilee].

- {Nation of Esau} = {Ten Horns} = [Ten kings = Ten tribes: *(Ephraim, Manasseh, Naphtali, Dan, Asher, Issachar, Zebulon, Simeon, Reuben, and Gad)* = Nation of Ephraim = *who are yet to receive a kingdom of their own* = Kingdom of Samaria = Conquered by the Assyrian Empire = Exodus by the Kushite Empire *(Wadi of Egypt)*] = [2ⁿᵈ Exodus] = {Descendants of Esau} = {Eastern hill country} = {Land of Samaria} = {Land of Israel} = {Land of the Gentiles} = [1ˢᵗ District of Galilee = District region of Nazareth *(Joseph, Mary and Jesus exiled)*] = [2ⁿᵈ District of Galilee = District region of Capernaum *(Land of Zebulun and land of Naphtali, the way to the sea, along the Jordan)*] = **[3ʳᵈ District of Galilee = District region of Bethsaida]**

- {Nation of Jacob} = {Beast} = [single tribe: *(Benjamin)* = Nation of Judah = *remained in the city* = Conquered by Babylonian Empire = Exodus by the Persian Empire] = [2ⁿᵈ Exodus] = [Kingdom of Jerusalem] = {Descendants of Jacob} = {Western hill country} = {Land of Jerusalem} = {Land of the Jews} = [Hill region of Judea: *(Zechariah and Elizabeth)*] = [Region of Judea: *(Joseph and Mary)*] = [Capital region of Jerusalem = Jerusalem the Holy City] = [Region of Bethany *(less than two miles from Jerusalem the Holy City)*]

{Important note2: If you look closely at the description of the verse, ***'Then they came to Capernaum. While Jesus was in the house, He asked them, "What were you arguing about on the road?'*** – Mark 9:33, you will discover it is a deceptive trap! At no time did Jesus ever live in the 2ⁿᵈ district of Galilee, the region called Capernaum. He merely, passes through the 2ⁿᵈ district to reach the 3ʳᵈ district}

The next thing you must do is re-list the entire descriptions removed from the verses and place the bold descriptions in the correct number order according to the context of the story.

> [4] **The next day Jesus decided to leave for** Galilee
>
> Philip, like Andrew and Peter, was from [5] **the town of Bethsaida**

Next, remove the bold descriptions in numbered order and reconstruct them into the correct context of the story as seen below,

> [4] The next day Jesus decided to leave for [5] the town of Bethsaida

To reveal the second piece to the sacred document of Immanuel you must merge the revelations into the correct context as seen below,

> [Leaving Nazareth *(1st district of Galilee)*, he went in Capernaum *(2nd district of Galilee)* Land of Zebulun and land of Naphtali, the way to the sea *(Sea of Galilee)*, along the Jordan *(Jordan River)*]
> **[The next day Jesus decided to leave for the town of Bethsaida *(3rd district of Galilee)*]**

The next thing you must do is look closely at the bold portion in the following description of John 1:44-45 below,

> [**Now Philip was from Bethsaida,** the same town as Andrew and Peter. **Philip found Nathanael and told him** We have found the One Moses wrote about in the Law, the One whom the prophets foretold **-Jesus of Nazareth, the son of Joseph."**]

(Note19: This description reveals another clue. For example: The clue is revealed by the number of natives Jesus meets that are natives from the same region. Thus far, Jesus meets two natives who are from the region of Bethsaida (Thus, Philip introduces Nathanael to Jesus))

The next thing you must do is merge the revelations together into the correct context.

- {Nation of Esau} = {Ten Horns} = [Ten kings = Ten tribes: *(Ephraim, Manasseh, Naphtali, Dan, Asher, Issachar, Zebulon, Simeon, Reuben, and Gad)* = Nation of Ephraim = *who are yet to receive a kingdom of their own* = Kingdom of Samaria = Conquered by the Assyrian Empire = Exodus by the Kushite Empire *(Wadi of Egypt)*] = [2nd Exodus] = {Descendants of Esau} = {Eastern hill country} = {Land of Samaria} = {Land of Israel} = {Land of the Gentiles} = [1st District of Galilee = District region of Nazareth *(Joseph, Mary and Jesus exiled)*] = [2nd District of Galilee = District region of Capernaum *(Land of Zebulun and land of Naphtali, the way to the sea, along the Jordan)*] = [3rd District of Galilee = District region of Bethsaida *(Philip and Nathanael)*]

- {Nation of Jacob} = {Beast} = [single tribe: *(Benjamin)* = Nation of Judah = *remained in the city* = Conquered by Babylonian Empire = Exodus by the Persian Empire] = [2nd Exodus] = [Kingdom of Jerusalem] = {Descendants of Jacob} = {Western hill country} = {Land of Jerusalem} = {Land of the Jews} = [Hill region of Judea: *(Zechariah and Elizabeth)*] = [Region of Judea: *(Joseph and Mary)*] = [Capital region of Jerusalem = Jerusalem the Holy City] = [Region of Bethany *(less than two miles from Jerusalem the Holy City)*]

The next thing you must do is re-list the entire descriptions removed from the verses and place the bold descriptions in the correct number order according to the context of the story.

[6] **Now Philip was from Bethsaida**, the same town as Andrew and Peter. **[7] Philip found Nathanael and told him** We have found the One Moses wrote about in the Law, the One whom the prophets foretold [8] **-Jesus of Nazareth, the son of Joseph."**

Next, remove the bold descriptions in numbered order and reconstruct them into the correct context of the story as seen below,

[6] Now Philip was from Bethsaida [7] Philip found Nathanael and told him [8]-Jesus of Nazareth, the son of Joseph."

To reveal the third piece to the sacred document of Immanuel you must merge the revelations into the correct context as seen below,

[Leaving Nazareth *(1st district of Galilee)*, he went in Capernaum *(2nd district of Galilee)* Land of Zebulun and land of Naphtali, the way to the sea *(Sea of Galilee)*, along the Jordan *(Jordan River)*] [The next day Jesus decided to leave for the town of Bethsaida *(3rd district of Galilee)*] **[Now Philip was from Bethsaida, Philip found Nathanael and told him -Jesus of Nazareth, the son of Joseph."]**

The next thing you must do is look carefully at the bold portion in the following descriptions below,

Matthew 4:18-20 - [**As Jesus was walking beside the Sea of Galilee, he saw two brothers. Simon called Peter and his brother Andrew. They were casting a net into the lake, for they were fishermen.** "Come, follow me," Jesus said, "and I will make you fishers of men." At once they left their nets and followed him]

Mark 1:16-18 - [**As Jesus walked beside the Sea of Galilee, he saw Simon and his brother Andrew casting a net into the lake, for they were fishermen.** "Come, follow me," Jesus said, "and I will make you fishers of men." At once they left their nets and followed him]

Luke 5:1-4 – [**One day as Jesus was standing by the lake of Gennesaret**, with the people crowding around him and listening to the word of God, **he saw at the water's edge two boats, left there by the fishermen, who were washing their nets. He got into one of the boats, the one belonging to Simon, and asked him to put out a little from shore.** Then he sat down and taught the people from the boat. When he had finished speaking, he said to Simon, **"Put out into deep water and let down the nets for a catch**]

Next, remove the following descriptions from the verses.

1- As Jesus was walking beside the Sea of Galilee, he saw two brothers. Simon called Peter and his brother Andrew

2- They were casting a net into the lake, for they were fishermen

3- As Jesus walked beside the Sea of Galilee, he saw Simon and his brother Andrew casting a net into the lake, for they were fishermen

4- One day as Jesus was standing by the lake of Gennesaret

5- he saw at the water's edge two boats, left there by the fishermen, who were washing their nets

6- He got into one of the boats, the one belonging to Simon, and asked him to put out a little from shore

7- Put out into deep water and let down the nets for a catch

Next, re-list the following descriptions removed from the verses.

- [As Jesus was walking beside the Sea of Galilee, he saw two brothers. Simon called Peter and his brother Andrew]
- [As Jesus walked beside the Sea of Galilee, he saw Simon and his brother Andrew casting a net into the lake, for they were fishermen]

(Note20: The next two natives Jesus meets in the region is Simon and his brother Andrew (fishermen). This brings the total number of natives to four!)

The next thing you must do is merge the revelations together into the correct context.

- {Nation of Esau} = {Ten Horns} = [Ten kings = Ten tribes: *(Ephraim, Manasseh, Naphtali, Dan, Asher, Issachar, Zebulon, Simeon, Reuben, and Gad)* = Nation of Ephraim = *who are yet to receive a kingdom of their own* = Kingdom of Samaria = Conquered by the Assyrian Empire = Exodus by the Kushite Empire *(Wadi of Egypt)*] = [2ⁿᵈ Exodus] = {Descendants of Esau} = {Eastern hill country} = {Land of Samaria} = {Land of Israel} = {Land of the Gentiles} = [1ˢᵗ District of Galilee = District region of Nazareth *(Joseph, Mary and Jesus exiled)*] = [2ⁿᵈ District of Galilee = District region of Capernaum *(Land of Zebulun and land of Naphtali, the way to the sea, along the Jordan)*] = [3ʳᵈ District of Galilee = District region of Bethsaida *(Philip, Nathanael, **Simon and Andrew**)*]

- {Nation of Jacob} = {Beast} = [single tribe: *(Benjamin)* = Nation of Judah = *remained in the city* = Conquered by Babylonian Empire = Exodus by the Persian Empire] = [2ⁿᵈ Exodus] = [Kingdom of Jerusalem] = {Descendants of Jacob} = {Western hill country} = {Land of Jerusalem} = {Land of the Jews} = [Hill region of Judea: *(Zechariah and Elizabeth)*] = [Region of Judea: *(Joseph and Mary)*] = [Capital region of Jerusalem = Jerusalem the Holy City]

Next, re-list the following descriptions removed from the verses.

- [He got into one of the boats, the one belonging to Simon, and asked him to put out a little from shore]
- [Put out into deep water and let down the nets for a catch]

(Note21: The following description 'Put out into deep water' reveals the next clue. For example: The 'shore region' in the following description 'put out a little from shore' corresponds to the shore region of Bethsaida, also known as the 3rd district of Galilee. However, the following description 'Put out into deep water' corresponds to another shore region that resides across from it. Thus, the Sea of Galilee represents a body of water that separates two district regions. The name and district of this shore region will reveal the mystery behind this description 'Put out into deep water.' To reveal the name and district you must locate another clue revealed in the next description below))

Next, re-list the following description removed from the verses.

- [One day as Jesus was standing by the lake of Gennesaret]

(Note22: This description 'by the lake of Gennesaret' is written deceptively! For example: The lake of Gennesaret is symbolic and represents what is called the shore region of Gennesaret. Thus, the Sea of Galilee does not represent a lake. Therefore, the district region of Bethsaida and the district region of Gennesaret represent two lands divided by the Sea of Galilee. The shore region of Gennesaret also reveals a hidden clue. Example2: The shore region of Gennesaret represents another district of Galilee (resides across the Sea from the 3rd district of Galilee), in the land of Samaria))

Here is the next clue: The following description 'Put out into deep water' corresponds to the shore region of Gennesaret and represents the following district of Galilee: [4th District of Galilee].

The next thing you must do is merge the revelations together into the correct context.

- {Nation of Esau} = {Ten Horns} = [Ten kings = Ten tribes: *(Ephraim, Manasseh, Naphtali, Dan, Asher, Issachar, Zebulon, Simeon, Reuben, and Gad)* = Nation of Ephraim = *who are yet to receive a kingdom of their own* = Kingdom of Samaria = Conquered by the Assyrian Empire = Exodus by the Kushite Empire *(Wadi of Egypt)*] = [2nd Exodus] = {Descendants of Esau} = {Eastern hill country} = {Land of Samaria} = {Land of Israel} = {Land of the Gentiles} = [1st District of Galilee = District region of Nazareth *(Joseph, Mary and Jesus exiled)*] = [2nd District of Galilee = District region of Capernaum *(Land of Zebulun and land of Naphtali, the way to the sea, along the Jordan)*] = [3rd District of Galilee = District region of Bethsaida *(Philip, Nathanael, Simon and Andrew)* = **Bethsaida Shore region of Galilee] = [4th District of Galilee = District region of Gennesaret = Gennesaret Shore region of Galilee]**

- {Nation of Jacob} = {Beast} = [single tribe: *(Benjamin)* = Nation of Judah = *remained in the city* = Conquered by Babylonian Empire = Exodus by the Persian Empire] = [2nd Exodus] = [Kingdom of Jerusalem] = {Descendants of Jacob} = {Western hill country} = {Land of Jerusalem} = {Land of the Jews} = [Hill region of Judea: *(Zechariah and Elizabeth)*] = [Region of Judea: *(Joseph and Mary)*] = [Capital region of Jerusalem = Jerusalem the Holy City] = [Region of Bethany *(less than two miles from Jerusalem the Holy City)*]

{**Important note3:** If you look closely at the following two descriptions ***'On the third day a wedding took place at Cana in Galilee. Jesus' mother was there, and Jesus and his disciples had also been invited to the wedding'*** – John 2:1-2, and ***'He came to Cana in Galilee, where he had turned the water into wine'*** - John 4:46, you will discover it too, is a deceptive trap! For example: There are four district regions of Galilee that collectively make up the entire land of the eastern hill country, the land of Samaria. These district regions are as follows: The region of Nazareth *(1st district of Galilee)*, The region of Capernaum *(2nd district of Galilee)*, The region of Bethsaida *(3rd district of Galilee)* and the region of Gennesaret *(4th district of Galilee)*. The four districts of Galilee, also called Galileans, collectively make up the entire land of Samaria, also called Samaritans. Thus, they also make up the entire land of the eastern hill country, the land of Israel, also called the land of the Gentiles. **Cana in Galilee** does not represent a district region of Galilee because the land of Samaria only consists of four district regions, not five! Therefore, a wedding never took place in Cana in Galilee because this region does not represent a district of Galilee, nor is it a region at all! Which means…, **Jesus never turned water into wine!**}

The next thing you must do is re-list the entire descriptions removed from the verses and place the bold descriptions in the correct number order according to the context of the story.

As Jesus was walking beside the Sea of Galilee, [11] - **he saw two brothers**.

[12] - **Simon** called Peter **and his brother Andrew**

They were casting a net into the lake, for they were fishermen

[9] - **As Jesus walked beside the Sea of Galilee**, he saw Simon and his brother Andrew casting a net into the lake, for they were fishermen

One day as Jesus was standing by the lake of Gennesaret

[10] - **he saw at the water's edge two boats, left there by the fishermen**, [13] - **who were washing their nets**

[15] - **He got into one of the boats, the one belonging to Simon**, [14] - **and asked him to put out a little from shore**

[16] - **Put out into deep water and let down the nets for a catch**

Next, remove the bold descriptions in numbered order and reconstruct them into the correct context of the story as seen below,

[9] - As Jesus walked beside the Sea of Galilee, [10] - he saw at the water's edge two boats, left there by the fishermen. [11] - He saw two brothers [12] - Simon and his brother Andrew, [13] - who were washing their nets [14] - and asked him to put out a little from shore. [15] - He got into one of the boats, the one belonging to Simon. [16] - Put out into deep water and let down the nets for a catch.'

To reveal the fourth piece to the sacred document of Immanuel you must merge the revelations into the correct context as seen below,

[Leaving Nazareth *(1st district of Galilee)*, he went in Capernaum *(2nd district of Galilee)* Land of Zebulun and land of Naphtali, the way to the sea *(Sea of Galilee)*, along the Jordan *(Jordan River)*] [The next day Jesus decided to leave for the town of Bethsaida *(3rd district of Galilee)*] [Now Philip was from Bethsaida, Philip found Nathanael and told him -Jesus of Nazareth, the son of Joseph."][**As Jesus walked beside the Sea of Galilee, *(accompanied by Philip and Nathanael)* he saw at the water's edge *(Bethsaida shore region)* two boats, left there by the fishermen *(companions of Philip and Nathanael)*. He saw two brothers - Simon and his brother Andrew, who were washing their nets and asked him to put out a little from shore *(sail beyond the Bethsaida shore region limit)*. He got into one of the boats, the one belonging to Simon *(accompanied by Andrew, Philip and Nathanael)*. Put out into deep water and let down the nets for a catch *(sail to the Gennesaret shore region)*]**

The next thing you must do is look closely at the bold portion in the following descriptions below,

Luke 5:9-10 - [For he and all **his companions were astonished at the catch of fish they had taken, and so were James and John, the sons of Zebedee, Simon's partners**]

Mark 1:19-20 - [**When he had gone a little farther, he saw James son of Zebedee and his brother John in a boat, preparing their nets.** Without delay he called them, and they left their father Zebedee in the boat with the hired men and followed him]

Matthew 4:21-22 - [**Going on from there, he saw two other brothers, James son of Zebedee and his brother John.** They were in a boat with their father Zebedee, preparing their nets. Jesus called them, and immediately they left the boat and their father and followed him]

Luke 5:7 – [**So they signaled their partners in the other boat to come and help them, and they came and filled both boats so full that they began to sink**]

Next, remove the following descriptions from the verses.

1- his companions were astonished at the catch of fish they had taken, and so were James and John, the sons of Zebedee, Simon's partners
2- When he had gone a little farther, he saw James son of Zebedee and his brother John in a boat, preparing their nets
3- Going on from there, he saw two other brothers, James son of Zebedee and his brother John
4- So they signaled their partners in the other boat to come and help them, and they came and filled both boats so full that they began to sink

(Note23: These descriptions reveal two major clues. For example: The next two natives Jesus meet is James and his brother John, the sons of Zebedee (also from Bethsaida). The second clue is the following: If you look closely at this description 'When he had gone a little farther, he saw James's son of Zebedee and his brother John in a boat, preparing their nets' you will discover that James and John are still within the border limits of the Bethsaida shore region))

59

*(Note24: If you look closely at this description 'So they signaled their partners in the other boat to come and help them' you will discover that Simon and Andrew sailed beyond the shore limits of James and John (thus, Simon and Andrew prepared their nets in the shore region of Gennesaret). This revelation corresponds to the following description – **'Put out into deep water and let down the nets for a catch.'))***

Here is the next clue: The next two natives Jesus meets from the region of Bethsaida are the following brothers: [James and John, the sons of Zebedee]

The next thing you must do is merge the revelations together into the correct context.

- {Nation of Esau} = {Ten Horns} = [Ten kings = Ten tribes: *(Ephraim, Manasseh, Naphtali, Dan, Asher, Issachar, Zebulon, Simeon, Reuben, and Gad)* = Nation of Ephraim = *who are yet to receive a kingdom of their own* = Kingdom of Samaria = Conquered by the Assyrian Empire = Exodus by the Kushite Empire *(Wadi of Egypt)*] = [2nd Exodus] = {Descendants of Esau} = {Eastern hill country} = {Land of Samaria} = {Land of Israel} = {Land of the Gentiles} = [1st District of Galilee = District region of Nazareth *(Joseph, Mary and Jesus exiled)*] = [2nd District of Galilee = District region of Capernaum *(Land of Zebulun and land of Naphtali, the way to the sea, along the Jordan)*] = [3rd District of Galilee = District region of Bethsaida *(Philip, Nathanael, Simon, Andrew, **James and John**)* = Bethsaida Shore region of Galilee] = [4th District of Galilee = District region of Gennesaret = Gennesaret Shore region of Galilee]

- {Nation of Jacob} = {Beast} = [single tribe: *(Benjamin)* = Nation of Judah = *remained in the city* = Conquered by Babylonian Empire = Exodus by the Persian Empire] = [2nd Exodus] = {Descendants of Jacob} = [Kingdom of Jerusalem] = {Western hill country} = {Land of Jerusalem} = {Land of the Jews} = [Hill region of Judea: *(Zechariah and Elizabeth)*] = [Region of Judea: *(Joseph and Mary)*] = [Capital region of Jerusalem = Jerusalem the Holy City] = [Region of Bethany *(less than two miles from Jerusalem the Holy City)*]

The next thing you must do is re-list the entire descriptions removed from the verses and place the bold descriptions in the correct number order according to the context of the story.

[21] - his companions were astonished at the catch of fish they had taken, [22] - and so were James and John, the sons of Zebedee, [23] - Simon's partners
[17] - When he had gone a little farther, he saw James son of Zebedee and his brother John **[19] - in a boat, preparing their nets**
[20] - Going on from there, [18] - he saw two other brothers, James son of Zebedee and his brother John
[24] - So they signaled their partners in the other boat to come and help them, and they came and filled both boats so full that they began to sink

Next, remove the bold descriptions in numbered order and reconstruct them into the correct context of the story as seen below,

[17] - When he had gone a little farther, he saw [18] - two other brothers, James son of Zebedee and his brother John [19] - in a boat, preparing their nets. [20] - Going on from there, [21] – his companions were astonished at the catch of fish they had taken, [22] – and so were James and John, the sons of Zebedee [23] - Simon's partners' [24] - So they signaled their partners in the other boat to come and help them, and they came and filled both boats so full that they began to sink

To reveal the fifth piece to the sacred document of Immanuel you must merge the revelations into the correct context as seen below,

[Leaving Nazareth *(1ˢᵗ district of Galilee)*, he went in Capernaum *(2ⁿᵈ district of Galilee)* Land of Zebulun and land of Naphtali, the way to the sea *(Sea of Galilee)*, along the Jordan *(Jordan River)*] [The next day Jesus decided to leave for the town of Bethsaida *(3ʳᵈ district of Galilee)*] [Now Philip was from Bethsaida, Philip found Nathanael and told him -Jesus of Nazareth, the son of Joseph."][As Jesus walked beside the Sea of Galilee, *(accompanied by Philip and Nathanael)* he saw at the water's edge *(Bethsaida shore region)* two boats, left there by the fishermen *(companions of Philip and Nathanael)*. He saw two brothers - Simon and his brother Andrew, who were washing their nets and asked him to put out a little from shore *(sail beyond the Bethsaida shore region limit)*. He got into one of the boats, the one belonging to Simon *(accompanied by Andrew, Philip and Nathanael)*. Put out into deep water and let down the nets for a catch *(sail to the Gennesaret shore region)*][**When he *(Simon)* had gone a little farther, he saw two other brothers, James's son of Zebedee and his brother John *(fishing companions)* in a boat, preparing their nets. Going on from there, *(crossing the Bethsaida border into the Gennesaret region)* his companions *(Simon, Andrew, Philip and Nathanael)* were astonished at the catch of fish they had taken, and so were James and John, the sons of Zebedee *(native companions from the Bethsaida region)* Simon's partners.' So they signaled their partners in the other boat *(James and John -sons of Zebedee)* to come and help them, and they came *(from Bethsaida shore region)* and filled both boats so full that they began to sink *(Gennesaret shore region)*]**

{**Important note4:** If Jesus and his companions are in the Sea of Galilee, in the Gennesaret shore region, and John the Baptist is said to have baptize Jesus in the Jordan River; where then is John the Baptist during the exact moment Jesus and his companions are hauling the nets of fish into the boats? To solve this mystery, you must shift away from the Path of Jesus and follow the Path of John, the son of Zechariah. Hidden behind the mystery will reveal a very important revelation}

THE PATH OF JOHN THE BAPTIST

The first thing you must do is look carefully at the bold portion in the following description of Luke 1:13.

[But the angel said to him: "**Do not be afraid, Zechariah; your prayer has been heard. Your wife Elizabeth will bear you a son, and you are to give him the name John**]

(Note25: This description reveals another major clue. For example: John is named after his father's house and will become known as John the son of Zechariah. Thus, John is also a native living in the hill region of Judea)

The next thing you must do is merge the revelations together into the correct context.

- {Nation of Esau} = {Ten Horns} = [Ten kings = Ten tribes: *(Ephraim, Manasseh, Naphtali, Dan, Asher, Issachar, Zebulon, Simeon, Reuben, and Gad)* = Nation of Ephraim = *who are yet to receive a kingdom of their own* = Kingdom of Samaria = Conquered by the Assyrian Empire = Exodus by the Kushite Empire *(Wadi of Egypt)*] = [2nd Exodus] = {Descendants of Esau} = {Eastern hill country} = {Land of Samaria} = {Land of Israel} = {Land of the Gentiles} = [1st District of Galilee = District region of Nazareth *(Joseph, Mary and Jesus exiled)*] = [2nd District of Galilee = District region of Capernaum *(Land of Zebulun and land of Naphtali, the way to the sea, along the Jordan)*] = [3rd District of Galilee = District region of Bethsaida *(Philip, Nathanael, Simon, Andrew, James and John)* = Bethsaida Shore region of Galilee] = [4th District of Galilee = District region of Gennesaret = Gennesaret Shore region of Galilee]

- {Nation of Jacob} = {Beast} = [single tribe: *(Benjamin)* = Nation of Judah = *remained in the city* = Conquered by Babylonian Empire = Exodus by the Persian Empire] = [2nd Exodus] = [Kingdom of Jerusalem] = {Descendants of Jacob} = {Western hill country} = {Land of Jerusalem} = {Land of the Jews} = [Hill country of Judea: *(Zechariah, Elizabeth and **John son of Zechariah**)*] = [Region of Judea: *(Joseph and Mary)*] = [Capital region of Jerusalem = Jerusalem the Holy City] = [Region of Bethany *(less than two miles from Jerusalem the Holy City)*]

The next thing you must do is look carefully at the bold portion in the following description of Luke 3:1-3.

[In the fifteenth year of the reign of Tiberius Caesar-When Pontius Pilate was governor of Judea, Herod tetrarch of Galilee, his brother Philip tetrarch of Iturea and Traconitis, and Lysanias tetrarch of Abilene-**during the high priesthood of Annas and Caiaphas, the word of God came to John son of Zechariah in the desert. He went into all the country around the Jordan, preaching a baptism of repentance for the forgiveness of sins**]

Next, remove the following description from the verses.

1- during the high priesthood of Annas and Caiaphas, the word of God came to John son of Zechariah in the desert
2- He went into all the country around the Jordan, preaching a baptism of repentance for the forgiveness of sins

Next, relist the following description removed from the verses,

- during the high priesthood of Annas and Caiaphas, the word of God came to John son of Zechariah in the desert

(Note26: There are two major clues revealed in the description above. The first clue for example is the following: The priesthood of Annas and Caiaphas also corresponds to the priestly division of Abijah (Luke 1:5) and represents the priestly division of Aaron. This revelation corresponds to the following description 'But only you and your sons may serve as priests in connection with everything at the altar and inside the curtain. I am giving you the service of the priesthood as a gift. Anyone else who comes near the sanctuary is to be put to death.'– Numbers 18:7. As previously revealed, Zechariah (John's father) belonged to the priestly division of Abijah (Thus, Abijah reigned over the priestly division in the time of Joseph, Mary, Elizabeth and Zechariah as well as Lorded over the land of the Jews). However, John does not belong to the priestly division of Abijah; but belongs to the priestly division of Annas and Caiaphas. This revelation corresponds to the following description '"Aaron's sacred garments will belong to his descendants so that they can be anointed and ordained in them' – 1ˢᵗ Chronicles 23:28. Annas and Caiaphas succeeded Abijah as High priests and now reigns over the priestly division in the time of John, the son of Zechariah as well as Lord over the land of the Jews. This revelation corresponds to the following two descriptions, 'Then the

detachment of soldiers with its commander and the Jewish officials arrested Jesus. They bound him and brought him first to Annas' – John 18:12-13 as well as *'Then Annas sent him bound to Caiaphas the high priest'* – John 18:24))

{**Important note5:** There is an unseen clue revealed by Abijah, Annas and Caiaphas *(Lord's over the land of the Jews)* that is revealed in the 1st Chronicle of the Elijah Doctrine *(Revelation of the Sign)*, regarding the Golden Calf and the Golden Calves. **For example: Abijah** *(reigned in the time of Joseph, Mary, Elizabeth and Zechariah)* **corresponds to the word 'Elder' and represents the Golden Calf, as the elder generation. Example2: Annas and Caiaphas** *(reigned in the time of John the son of Zechariah)* **corresponds to the word 'descendant' and represents the Golden Calves, as the descendant generation.** Thus, Abijah *(Chief priest)* corresponds to the Golden Calf *(Lord over the elder generation of Jews)*; and Annas and Caiaphas *(High priests)* corresponds to the Golden Calves *(Lords over the descendant generation of Jews)*}

{**Important note6:** Annas and Caiaphas also reveals the great deception behind this verse *'But when he heard that Archelaus was reigning in Judea in place of his father Herod'* - Matthew 2:22. For example: The deception is revealed by this description *'They bound him and brought him first to Annas, who was the father-in-law of Caiaphas'* – John 18:12. Thus, there is a paradox revealed by the two descriptions that reveals the great deception. To understand this, you must merge the two descriptions together to see the paradox. Example2: The name <u>Herod</u> *(in place of his father)* and <u>Annas</u> *(who was the father-in-law)* is symbolic and corresponds to the word '<u>Elder</u>.' Thus, Herod, is a deceptive trap and does not belong and corresponds to Annas the high priest. On the other hand, <u>Archelaus</u> *(son of Herod)* and <u>Caiaphas</u> *(son-in-law of Annas)* is symbolic and corresponds to the word '<u>Descendant</u>.' Thus, Archelaus, is another deceptive trap and does not belong and corresponds to Caiaphas the high priest. Therefore, the name Herod *(reigned in Judea)* corresponds to Annas the high priest *(Lord over the land of Jerusalem)* and Archelaus *(reigned in Judea)* corresponds to Caiaphas the high priest *(Lord over the land of Jerusalem)*}

(Note27: The second clue for example is the following: As previously revealed, Zechariah belongs to the priestly division of Aaron and represents a descendant of Aaron. Thus, John the son of Zechariah also belongs to the priestly division of Aaron and represents a descendant of Aaron (for he is the son of a priest). Therefore, John must be raised to walk in his father's footsteps (continues the priestly line of Aaron). This revelation reveals the meaning behind the following description 'The priest who is anointed and ordained to succeed his father as high priest is to make atonement. He is to put on the sacred linen

*garments' – Leviticus 16:32. The mystery of both clues is revealed behind the understanding of this description **'When he was twelve years old.'** To reveal the mystery, you must bring back the previous description of Luke 2:41-43)*

Look closely at the previous descriptions below regarding Luke 2:41-43 below,

- Every year his parents went to Jerusalem for the Feast of the Passover
- When he was twelve years old, they went up to the Feast, according to the custom
- the boy Jesus stayed behind in Jerusalem

*(Note28: These descriptions above reveal four major clues. These clues correspond to the previous revelations regarding the priestly division of Abijah, Annas, and Caiaphas. For example: After a male child is born, it is the custom of the Jews during the eighth day to present him in Jerusalem, the Holy City, to partake in the ceremonial purification of Circumcision. Thus, the boy in this description of Luke 2:21 – 'On the eighth day, when it was time to circumcise him' does not correspond to Jesus (born to Mary and Joseph); but represents John, son of Zechariah (born to Elizabeth and Zechariah). Jesus would have remained uncircumcised according to the custom of the Gentiles, the land of the eastern hill country. The reason is revealed by this description **'You are well aware that it is against our law for a Jew to associate with or visit a Gentile'** – Acts 10:28. Thus, no native from the eastern hill country, the land of the Gentiles, would enter the land of the western hill country, the land of Jerusalem, to partake in the ceremonial purification of circumcision in keeping with the Law of Moses, in Jerusalem the Holy City, as is the custom of the Jews))*

*(Note29: The parents in the description of Luke 2:41 – 'Every year his parents went to Jerusalem for the Feast of the Passover' does not correspond to Mary and Joseph; but represents Elizabeth and Zechariah. For example: Jesus and his parents remained in exile to the land of Israel (the eastern hill country, the land of the Gentiles) and continued to reside in the 1st district of Galilee called Nazareth. Thus, Jesus would be raised in the custom of the Gentiles; not in the custom of the Jews (thus, he will be called a Nazarene, a Galilean, a Samaritan, and a Gentile). Therefore, he will not be called a Jew, nor a descendant from the house and line of David. This revelation corresponds to the following description 'Our ancestors worshiped on this mountain (eastern hill country land), but you Jews claim that the place where we must worship is in Jerusalem (western hill country land) – John 4:20.' This revelation is further confirmed by the following description **'For Jews do not associate with Samaritans'** – John 4:9. Thus, at*

no time, did Jesus ever attend the Feast of the Passover! Therefore, the parents in the description of Luke 2:41, corresponds to Zechariah and Elizabeth (every year attended the Feast of the Passover according to the custom of the Jews))

*(Note30: The boy in the description of Luke 2:42 – 'When he was twelve years old' does not correspond to Jesus (born to Mary and Joseph); but represents John, son of Zechariah (born to Elizabeth and Zechariah). For example: The 'age of twelve' is symbolic and reveals an important revelation that will be uncovered by understanding the bold portion of this description 'the boy Jesus **stayed behind in Jerusalem**.' Example2: This part of the description 'stayed behind in Jerusalem' is symbolic and corresponds to the capital region city, known as Jerusalem the Holy City. Example3: When a male child (descendant of Aaron) reaches twelve years of age, he must be presented before the Temple courts to make preparation to succeed his father as High priest, as is the custom of the priestly division of Aaron (the child shall enter the school of the priesthood). This revelation corresponds to the following description – 'The priest who is anointed and ordained to succeed his father as high priest is to make atonement. He is to put on the sacred linen garments' – Leviticus 16:32. Thus, at no time, was Jesus (twelve years of age), ever presented before the Temple courts, in Jerusalem the Holy City. At the age of twelve, John, son of Zechariah becomes a priest and is presented before the priestly division presided over by Annas and Caiaphas. Therefore, John must remain behind in the region's Capital City, Jerusalem the Holy City, to fulfill his duties according to all that is required by the priestly division of Aaron. As a descendant of Aaron, John must be presented before Annas and Caiaphas. Example4: John, corresponds to this description '**went up to the temple courts and began to teach** – John 7:14-15 (thus, it is not Jesus who is left behind in Jerusalem the Holy City). Thus, at the age of twelve, Jesus remains in exile to the 1st district of Galilee, the region of Nazareth, in the eastern hill country, the land of Samaria. Example5: Mary and Joseph could not present Jesus before the Temple courts (at the age of twelve) because Jesus was not born a descendant of Aaron (cannot succeed his father as High priest by entering the school of the priesthood according to the Law of Moses). And so, only a descendant of Aaron can enter the Temple or be presented before the Temple courts. This revelation is further confirmed by the bold part of this description - 'Once when Zechariah's division was on duty and he was serving as priest before God, **he was chosen by lot, according to the custom of the priesthood, to go into the temple of the Lord and burn incense. And when the time for the burning of incense came, all the assembled worshipers were praying outside**' – Luke 1:8-9. Therefore, Jesus (not a descendant of Aaron, nor raised in the custom of the Jews) could not go up to the Temple courts and began to teach for this would be against the custom of the Jews and a violation of Law, as revealed by this description 'You are well aware that it is against our law for a Jew to associate with or visit a Gentile' – Acts 10:28.)*

Here is the next clue: **John the Baptist** corresponds to **John, son of Zechariah** *(descendant of Aaron)* and represents the following **twelve-year-old boy** that remained behind in Jerusalem the Holy City: [John the Levite].

*(Note31: A **Levite** represents an ordained priest who enters the school of the priesthood as is the custom of the priestly division of Aaron. The sacred duties of a Levite priest as a descendant of Aaron, is to continue the priestly line by one day succeeding his father as high priest. Thus, all male children (descendant of Aaron) must be presented before the Temple courts and are required by the Law of Moses to make preparation to succeed his father as high priest (this does not apply to the Jews who belong to the house and line of David). This revelation corresponds to the bold part of this description 'You shall have the Levites stand before Aaron and before his sons as to present them as a wave offering to the LORD. **"Thus you shall separate the Levites from among the sons of Israel, and the Levites shall be Mine'** – Numbers 8:14. It is for this reason that only a descendant of Aaron can enter the Temple or be presented before the temple courts. Thus, separating the descendants of Aaron from the House and line of David (the descendants of Judah). This revelation reveals why Zechariah, Elizabeth, and John, the son of Zechariah represents a descendant of Aaron. And why, Joseph, and Mary only belongs to the house and line of David (represents a descendant from the line of Judah))*

{**Important note7**: There is a hidden clue revealed behind the revelation of the word '**Baptist!**' The word 'Baptist' does not correspond to John the son of Zechariah; but corresponds to Abijah, the Chief priest, and Annas and Caiaphas, the high priest *(baptizes all male descendants of Aaron, a Levite)*. Thus, the word 'Baptist' represents one who baptizes. There is a hidden clue revealed in this description '*I baptize you with water for repentance*' – Matthew 3:11. The hidden clue is revealed by the understanding of the word '**Baptism!**' For Example: The word 'Baptism' does not correspond to 'water baptism.' On the contrary, it corresponds to 'oil baptism!' Example2: When a descendant of Aaron undergoes baptism, the ritual is conducted with oil, not with water! When water is used, the method is to wash the body before the ritual of baptism is conducted. The full ritual of baptism according to the priestly division of Aaron is revealed by this description '*Then bring Aaron and his sons to the entrance to the tent of meeting and wash them with water. Take the garments and dress Aaron with the tunic, the robe of the ephod, the ephod itself and the breast piece. Fasten the ephod on him by its skillfully woven waistband. Put the turban on his head and attach the sacred emblem to the turban. Take the anointing oil and anoint him by pouring it on his head. Bring his sons and dress them in tunics and fasten caps on them. Then tie sashes on Aaron*

and his sons. *The priesthood is theirs by a lasting ordinance.* <u>**Then you shall ordain Aaron and his sons'**</u> – Exodus 29:4-9. The words 'Baptize,' and 'Baptism' corresponds to the following ritual 'to anoint' and 'be anointed.' The completion of the ritual is revealed by the word 'ordained' *(becomes a Levite priest).* This revelation reveals the meaning behind this description <u>***'The priest who is anointed and ordained to succeed his father as High priest is to make atonement.*** <u>*He is to put on the sacred linen garments'*</u></u> – Leviticus 16:32. Thus, the word '<u>repentance</u>' corresponds to the word '<u>atonement</u>.' This revelation also reveals the meaning behind this description '"<u>***Aaron's sacred garments***</u> *will belong to his descendants so that they can be <u>anointed</u> and <u>ordained</u> in them'* – 1ˢᵗ Chronicles 23:28. Therefore, at the age of twelve, John the son of Zechariah, must leave his father's house *(remain behind in Jerusalem the Holy City)*, and is baptized a Levite priest by Annas and Caiaphas before the Temple courts *(enters the school of the priesthood).* The revelation revealed by the ritual of Baptism *(he is to put on the sacred linen garments)* reveals this description *'**John wore clothing made of camel's hair, with a leather belt around his waist'** –* Mark 1:6, to be another deceptive trap, because as John advances in age *(while in the school of the priesthood),* would have worn the garments of the Levites *(dressed in a tunic, a fasten cap, and a sash tied around his waist).* Thus, Abijah *(Chief priest)*, and Annas and Caiaphas *(High priests)* would have also worn the following sacred garments *(dressed in a tunic, the robe of the ephod, the breast piece, a skillfully woven waistband, the turban on their head, attached with the sacred emblem)*}

The next thing you must do is merge the revelations together into the correct context.

- {Nation of Esau} = {Ten Horns} = [Ten kings = Ten tribes: *(Ephraim, Manasseh, Naphtali, Dan, Asher, Issachar, Zebulon, Simeon, Reuben, and Gad)* = Nation of Ephraim = *who are yet to receive a kingdom of their own* = Kingdom of Samaria = Conquered by the Assyrian Empire = Exodus by the Kushite Empire *(Wadi of Egypt)*] = [2nd Exodus] = {Descendants of Esau} = {Eastern hill country} = {Land of Samaria} = {Land of Israel} = {Land of the Gentiles} = [1st District of Galilee = District region of Nazareth *(Joseph, Mary and Jesus exiled)*] = [2nd District of Galilee = District region of Capernaum *(Land of Zebulun and land of Naphtali, the way to the sea, along the Jordan)*] = [3rd District of Galilee = District region of Bethsaida *(Philip, Nathanael, Simon, Andrew, James and John)* = Bethsaida Shore region of Galilee] = [4th District of Galilee = District region of Gennesaret = Gennesaret Shore region of Galilee]

- {Nation of Jacob} = {Beast} = [single tribe: *(Benjamin)* = Nation of Judah = *remained in the city* = Conquered by Babylonian Empire = Exodus by the Persian Empire] = [2nd Exodus] = [Kingdom of Jerusalem] = {Descendants of Jacob} = {Western hill country} = {Land of Jerusalem} = {Land of the Jews} = [Hill country of Judea: *(Zechariah, Elizabeth and John son of Zechariah)*] = [Region of Judea: *(Joseph and Mary)*] = [Capital region of Jerusalem = Jerusalem the Holy City: ***(John becomes a Levite priest before the Temple courts)***] = [Region of Bethany *(less than two miles from Jerusalem the Holy City)*]

Next, relist the final description removed from the verses,

- He went into all the country around the Jordan, preaching a baptism of repentance for the forgiveness of sins

{**Important note8:** If you look closely at this description *'He went into all the country around the Jordan'* you will discover another deceptive trap! For example: The word 'country' corresponds to the eastern hill country, the land of Samaria. This description 'around the Jordan' corresponds to the 2nd district of Galilee, the district region called Capernaum *(along the Jordan River)*. The trap is revealed by the fact that Capernaum represents a district of Galilee, not a country of its own *(the only region of Galilee that resides by the Jordan River)*. This revelation is revealed by the bold part of this description *'Land of Zebulun and land of Naphtali, the way to the sea (Sea of Galilee), along the Jordan (Jordan River), Galilee (2nd district of Galilee) of the Gentiles (region called Capernaum)'* - Matthew 4:13-16}

{**Important note9:** If you look closely at this description *'preaching a baptism of repentance for the forgiveness of sins'* you will discover it too, is a deceptive trap! This revelation will be revealed in more detail shortly}

The next thing you must do is look closely at the bold portion in the following descriptions below,

Matthew 3:1 - [In those days **John the Baptist came, preaching in the Desert of Judea**]

Mark 1:4 - [And so **John came, baptizing in the desert region** and preaching a baptism of repentance for the forgiveness of sins]

Luke 1:80 - [And the child grew and became strong in spirit; and **he lived in the desert until he appeared publicly to Israel**]

Next, remove the following descriptions from the verses.

1- John the Baptist came, preaching in the Desert of Judea
2- John came, baptizing in the desert region
3- he lived in the desert until he appeared publicly to Israel

(Note33: These descriptions above are deceptively written. For example: John does not come preaching in the Desert of Judea (was born in the hill region of Judea, which borders the 1ˢᵗ district of Galilee called the region of Nazareth). John does not come baptizing in the desert (but is baptized a Levite priest before the Temple courts at the age of twelve). And John does not appear publicly to Israel (the eastern hill country, the land of Samaria), but appears publicly before Annas and Caiaphas in Jerusalem the Holy City (region of the western hill country). This revelation also corresponds to the description 'went up to the temple courts and began to teach – John 7:14-15. This revelation will be revealed in more detail shortly)

The next thing you must do is look closely at the following description below,

John 1:28 – [This all happened at Bethany on the other side of the Jordan, where John was baptizing]

*(Note34: The next clue is revealed behind this description '**This all happened at Bethany on the other side of the Jordan**.' For example: The other side of the Jordan River does not correspond to the region called Bethany. The following two lands that are divided by the Jordan River represents the lands known as Zebulun and Naphtali (along the Jordan River). These two lands make-up the 2nd district of Galilee, known as the region of Capernaum, which resides in the eastern hill country, known as the Land of Samaria (the land of the Gentiles))*

*(Note35: On the contrary, the region of Bethany represents a region that resides in the western hill country land, known as the Land of Jerusalem (the land of the Jews). The region of Bethany represents the next region that resides outside of Jerusalem the Holy City (traveling west toward the border of Egypt). This revelation corresponds to the following description 'Now Bethany was less than two miles from Jerusalem' – John 11:18 (Jerusalem being symbolic for representing Jerusalem the Holy City). Thus, Bethany does not reside by the Jordan River, nor, in the 2nd district of Galilee, known as Capernaum, nor does it reside in the land of the eastern hill country, known as the land of Samaria. As revealed previously, when the Magi from the east came to Jerusalem they would have first appeared before Abijah, not King Herod (See page 66). Thus, King Herod, Lords over the land of the eastern hill country, the land of Samaria. This revelation corresponds to the following description 'When he learned that Jesus was under Herod's jurisdiction, he sent him to Herod' – Luke 23:7. Therefore, the Magi (leaving Abijah the Chief priest) would have continued their journey less than two miles traveling in the western direction (west of the Holy City). This revelation corresponds to the following description '**After they had heard the king** (Abijah the Chief priest)**, they went on their way** (traveling west of the city towards the region of Bethany)' – Matthew 2:9. This revelation is revealed by the direction in which the star, they had seen in the east, went ahead of them (thus, during the summer solstice the Sun sets towards the land of the west). Therefore, the next region land outside of Jerusalem the Holy City (when continuing west of the city) is the region called Bethany (boarders the land of Egypt))*

The next thing you must do is look closely at the bold portion in the following description below,

John 1:19 – [Now this was John's testimony when **the Jews of Jerusalem sent priests and Levites** to ask him who he was]

*(Note36: This description reveals a great deception as well as a major clue. For example: John the Levite represents a descendant of Aaron. Thus, the Jews of Jerusalem (in the description above) refers to Annas and Caiaphas (also descendants of Aaron), and Lords over the land of Jerusalem. Therefore, this part of the description 'to ask him who he was,' is incorrect! It is incorrect, for this reason, all male children, a descendant of Aaron, who is required by Law to succeed his father as High priest are recorded in the genealogy of the Levites. This revelation corresponds to the bold portion of this description 'As for the priests, the descendants of Aaron, who lived on the farmlands around their towns or in any other towns, men were designated by name to distribute portions to every male among them **and to all who were recorded in the genealogies of the Levites'** – 2 Chronicles 31:19. It is for this reason, all male children, a descendant of Aaron, must be presented in Jerusalem, the Holy City, to fulfill his duties before the Temple courts, in keeping with the Law of Moses. The clue, however, is revealed behind the reason as to why the Jews of Jerusalem (also known as Annas and Caiaphas, the Lords of the land) sent priests and Levites (as representing the temple guards) to seek out John the Levite))*

(Note37: The first clue is revealed by the following: During the priestly division of Annas and Caiaphas, John the Levite rebels against his father's house! Thus, his father's house does not correspond to the house of Zechariah; but represents the house of the priestly division of Aaron, also known as the house of his fathers. This revelation will be revealed in more detail moving forward)

The next thing you must do is look closely at the bold portion of the description below,

Mark 6:17-18 – [For Herod himself had given orders to have John arrested, and he had him bound and put in prison. **He did this because of Herodias, his brother Philip's wife, whom he had married. For John had been saying to Herod, "It is not lawful for you to have your brother's wife."**]

(Note38: This description is written deceptively and reveals another trap! For example: Herod did not arrest John because he spoke out concerning the marriage of his brother's wife. There is another reason as to why Herod ordered John's arrest. The true revelation will disprove the following description – ***'So Herodias nursed a grudge against John and wanted to kill him. But she was not able to, because Herod feared John and protected him, knowing him to be a righteous and holy man.*** *When Herod heard John, he was greatly puzzled; yet he liked to listen to him' – Mark 6:19-20. Example2: John the son of Zechariah (also known as John the Levite) a native from the land of Jerusalem would not have had any association with Herod over Herodias, his brother Philip's wife, for the reason the Jews (land of the western hill country) do not associate with Samaritans, also called a Gentile (land of the eastern hill country). Thus, Herod Lords over the land of the eastern hill country, the land of Samaria and John is a native Jew from the land of Jerusalem, the western hill country. This revelation is revealed by the following description 'You are well aware that it is against our law for a Jew to associate with or visit a Gentile' – Acts 10:28. Therefore, John would not have had any association with Herod outside of his observance regarding his dealings with Annas and Caiaphas. The revelation regarding the arrest of John will be revealed in more detail moving forward. For now, you must find where the next set of clues are hidden))*

The next thing you must do is look closely at the bold portions of the following two descriptions below,

> **Acts 12:11** – [Then Peter came to himself and said, "Now I know for sure that the Lord has sent His angel **and rescued me from Herod's grasp and from everything the Jewish people were anticipating."**]

> Luke 23:7 – [When he learned that Jesus was under Herod's jurisdiction, **he sent him to Herod, who was also in Jerusalem at that time**]

*(Note39: If you look closely at the two descriptions you will notice where the clues are hidden. For example: Herod has jurisdiction in the land of the eastern hill country, the land of Samaria (land of the Gentiles). He does not have jurisdiction in the land of the western hill country, the land of Jerusalem (land of the Jews). Example2: If you look closely at this description 'You are well aware that it is against our law for a Jew to associate with or visit a Gentile' – Acts 10:28, you will discover how this description 'to Herod, who was also in Jerusalem at that time' reveals a conflict of interest between the two lands and considered by some in the western hill country a violation of Law, for this reason, Herod has no jurisdiction in the land of the western hill country, the land of Jerusalem. This revelation reveals the meaning behind this description '__For Jews do not associate with Samaritans__' – John 4:9. The next clue is revealed behind the understanding of this description 'rescued me from Herod's grasp and from everything the Jewish people were anticipating.' Example3: This description is symbolic and reveals a clue into how Annas and Caiaphas (lords over the land of Jerusalem), conspired with Herod (lord over the land of Samaria). Thus, upon Herod's return to the land of the western hill country, the land of Jerusalem, it was in the capital region city, Jerusalem the Holy City, where Annas and Caiaphas conspired with Herod in secret inside the Temple courts. The revelation into what they conspired over will be revealed in detail moving forward. Example4: If you look back at this description 'to Herod, who was also in Jerusalem at that time' you will discover the clue. John the Levite rebels against Annas and Caiaphas, the Lords of the land, because he saw their dealings with Herod as corrupt and a direct violation of the law as revealed by this description '__it is against our law for a Jew to associate with or visit a Gentile.__' His direct opposition to them breaking the law forced him to rebel against the house of his father's. If you look closely at the bold part of this description - 'On reaching Jerusalem, Jesus **entered the temple courts and began driving out those who were buying and selling there. He overturned the tables of the money changers and the benches of those selling doves and would not allow anyone to carry merchandise through the temple courts**' – Mark 11:15-16, you will discover, on the contrary, it was not Jesus who spoke out concerning the*

corruption taking place inside the Temple courts, it was John the Levite, who spoke out boastfully against the corruption of Annas and Caiaphas. Therefore, John does not rebel against Herod over Herodias, his brother Philip's wife (from the land of the Gentiles), because he would not have had any association with Herod, his brother Philip, nor Herodias, his wife (For Jews do not associate with Samaritans – John 4:9). Instead, he only rebelled by speaking out forcefully against Annas and Caiaphas, because he saw their hypocrisy and corruption, they allowed in the Temple courts and throughout the Holy City. This revelation also corresponds to this description **'The Pharisees heard the crowd whispering such things about him. Then the chief priests and the Pharisees sent temple guards to arrest him'** *– John 7:32. Thus, this description does not refer to Jesus, but refers to John, the Levite. The chief priests and Pharisees are also symbolic and refers to Annas and Caiaphas (High priests), the Lords of the land. The reason John the Levite goes into exile is because Annas and Caiaphas sent the Temple guards to secure his arrest for speaking out against them because of their corrupt dealings. This revelation reveals the meaning behind this description* **'he said to them: "You brood of vipers!** *– Matthew 3:7. Therefore, John escapes Annas and Caiaphas by fleeing away from Jerusalem the Holy City, before the Temple guards could secure his arrest, returns to his native region, the hill region of Judea, and leaves his native land by going into exile to the land of Israel (the eastern hill country, the land of Samaria). John the Levite journeys to the 1st district of Galilee, the region called Nazareth, to seek out his exiled relatives, Joseph, Mary, and Jesus. However, Jesus is no longer in the region of Nazareth when John arrives! Thus, John leaves the region of Nazareth to seek out his relative Jesus)*

Here is the next question. To which of the four districts of Galilee: Nazareth, Capernaum, Bethsaida or Gennesaret that makes up the eastern hill country, the land of Israel, the land of Samaria, is John the Levite standing when he sees his relative Jesus before he is arrested in the land? Within one of the four districts of Galilee, reveals the exact location as to where John the Levite is standing the moment Jesus and his companions are hauling the nets of fish into the boats. To uncover this mystery, you must locate another vital clue hidden behind the understanding of the bold part of this description 'you shall see heaven open, **and the angels of God ascending and descending on the Son of Man!'**

ANGELS OF GOD ASCENDING AND DESCENDING

The next thing you must do is look carefully at the bold portion in the following descriptions below,

John 1:51 – [I tell you the truth, **you shall see heaven open, and the angels of God ascending and descending on the Son of Man**]

Matthew 3:16 – [**As soon as Jesus was baptized, he went up out of the water. At that moment heaven was opened, and he saw the Spirit of God descending like a dove and lighting on him**]

John 1:32-33 – [**I saw the Spirit come down from heaven as a dove and remain on him. I would not have known him, except that the one who sent me to baptize with water told me, "The man on whom you see the Spirit come down and remain is he who will baptize with the Holy Spirit**]

Next, remove the following descriptions from the verses.

1- you shall see heaven open, and the angels of God ascending and descending on the Son of Man
2- As soon as Jesus was baptized, he went up out of the water
3- At that moment heaven was opened, and he saw the Spirit of God descending like a dove and lighting on him
4- I saw the Spirit come down from heaven as a dove and remain on him
5- I would not have known him, except that the one who sent me to baptize with water told me
6- The man on whom you see the Spirit come down and remain is he who will baptize with the Holy Spirit

Next, re-list the following descriptions removed from the verses below,

- you shall see heaven open, and the angels of God ascending and descending on the Son of Man
- At that moment heaven was opened, and he saw the Spirit of God descending like a dove and lighting on him
- The man on whom you see the Spirit come down and remain is he who will baptize with the Holy Spirit

*(Note40: The following descriptions above reveal a major clue. For example: The **Spirit or angels of God ascending, and descending** are symbolic and corresponds to the place where Jesus and his companions are hauling the nets of fish into their boats. The clue is revealed in the descriptions of Leviticus and Deuteronomy)*

Look closely at the following descriptions below,

Leviticus 11:16 – [the horned owl, the screech owl, the gull, any kind of hawk]

Deuteronomy 14:15 – [the horned owl, the screech owl, the gull, any kind of hawk]

*(Note41: The clue is revealed behind the revelation of the gull birds. The **'gull birds'** migrate near or around the Sea of Galilee. Thus, they are extremely attracted to fish. The gull bird is also known to resemble the likeness of a dove bird as it ascends and descends upon the fish)*

Here is the next clue: The Spirit or angels of God ascending and descending corresponds to the gull bird and represents the following bird that migrates around the Sea of Galilee: [The White gull bird].

*(Note42: The **white gull birds** are ascending and descending upon the boats of Simon and Andrew, and their companions James and John the sons of Zebedee. The white gull birds migrate around the Sea of Galilee in both district shore regions, known as Bethsaida and Gennesaret. Thus, they are attracted by the nets of fish being hauled into the boats in the Gennesaret Shore region of Galilee when John sees his relative Jesus hauling the net full of fish into the boat)*

79

Next, re-list the other following descriptions removed from the verses below,

- I would not have known him, except that the one who sent me to baptize with water told me
- The man on whom you see the Spirit come down and remain is he who will baptize with the Holy Spirit

(Note43: The following descriptions above reveal another major clue. For example: How does John, son of Zechariah know to recognize Jesus? If you look closely at the description of Luke 1:36 – 'Even Elizabeth your relative is going to have a child in her old age,' you will discover the hidden clue. Example2: Jesus the Nazarene and John the son of Zechariah are blood cousins. Thus, John is the elder cousin to Jesus. Jesus and John are exactly six months apart in age (Mary stayed with Elizabeth three months and then returned home – Luke 1:56). Though John did not grow up knowing Jesus, he could recognize a resemblance of himself. Therefore, John could recognize Jesus because the two share a resembling facial likeness. This revelation reveals the meaning behind the bold portion of this description '__When he saw Jesus passing by__, he said, "Look, the Lamb of God!" – John 1:36.' Thus, the 'Lamb of God' does not refer to Jesus, nor does it refer to a man. See the illustration below, as indicated in the 1ˢᵗ Chronicle of the Elijah Doctrine (Revelation of the Sign))

To illustrate this, bring back the revelation revealed by the 5ᵗʰ prominent horn and see how the **"Lamb of God"** corresponds to the 5ᵗʰ living creature as corresponding to the 5ᵗʰ beast and represents a woman:

- [5ᵗʰ prominent horn] = [8ᵗʰ king *(And from His mouth proceeds a sharp sword)*] = [Someone like a son of man *(will hate the prostitute)* = Man clothed in linen *(writing kit at his side)* = He came and took the scroll from the right hand of him who sat on the throne! = The armies of heaven were following him, riding on white horses and dressed in fine linen, white and clean] = [Solid gold lampstand] = [**5ᵗʰ beast = 5ᵗʰ living creature = Lamb looking as if slain = Woman**]

*(Note44: If you look closely at this description '**The man on whom you see the Spirit come down and remain**' (as referring to the Jordan River) reveals another major deception. For example: When John sees the spirit of God ascending and descending upon Jesus; he sees the **White gull birds ascending and descending** upon his relative in the Sea of Galilee (not in the Jordan River). Thus, John is somewhere nearby in one of the following two district regions: 'The district shore region of Bethsaida' or 'The district shore region of Gennesaret' (two district regions divided by the Sea of Galilee))*

Here is the final clue: **John the Levite** sees **white gull birds** ascending and descending upon his cousin Jesus *(hauling the net of fish into the boat)*, from the following district shore region of Galilee: [4th district of Galilee, the district region called Gennesaret].

{**Important note10:** If you look closely at the description of the verses, *'Then Jesus came from Galilee to the Jordan to be baptized by John. But John tried to deter him, saying, "I need to be baptized by you, and do you come to me?" Jesus replied, "Let it be so now; it is proper for us to do this to fulfill all righteousness." Then John consented'* – Matthew 3:13-15, you will discover it is a deceptive trap! Jesus does not leave Nazareth and enter the 2nd district of Galilee, the region called Capernaum, to be baptized by John the Levite. In fact, the two never got a chance to meet in the land of the eastern hill country before John is arrested *(though it was John who sought out his relative Jesus when he exiled himself from the land of the western hill country, the land of Jerusalem)*}

{**Important note11:** If you look closely at the description of the verses, *'Again they tried to seize him, but he escaped their grasp. Then Jesus went back across the Jordan to the place where John had been baptizing in the early days. There he stayed, and many people came to him. They said, "Though John never performed a sign, all that John said about this man was true." And in that place many believed in Jesus'* – John 10:39-42, you will discover it too, is a deceptive trap! For example: Jesus never stayed or lived in the 2nd district of Galilee, the region called Capernaum, nor does he return to the 2nd district of Galilee, after entering the 3rd district of Galilee, the region called Bethsaida. This revelation will be revealed in more detail moving forward. Example2: John the Levite, a native of the western hill country, the land of Jerusalem, did not associate with the people of the eastern hill country, the land of Samaria, before he exiled himself *(for Jews do not associate with Samaritans – John 4:9)*. Therefore, John the Levite would not have had any affiliation with the citizens of the 2nd district of Galilee, nor did he frequent the region called Capernaum *(it is against our law for a Jew to associate with or visit a Gentile – Acts 10:28)*}

Next, re-list the final description removed from the verses as seen below,

- As soon as Jesus was baptized, he went up out of the water

(Note45: This description is deceptive and reveals another trap! For example: John does not see White gull birds (spirits of God) ascending and descending upon Jesus in the 2ⁿᵈ district of Galilee, known as Capernaum (along the Jordan River), nor does John the Levite baptize Jesus in the Sea of Galilee, the shore region of Gennesaret. There are two clues hidden in the description of John 3:26 and John 1:26-28 that will further confirm why!)

Look closely at the bold portion in the following description below,

John 3:26 - [They came to John and said to him, "Rabbi, **that man who was with you on the other side of the Jordan**--the one you testified about--well, he is baptizing, and everyone is going to him]

(Note46: John does not encounter Jesus from either of the following two lands that make-up the 2ⁿᵈ district of Galilee, known as Zebulun and Naphtali (divided by the Jordan River). These two lands collectively represent the 2ⁿᵈ district of Galilee, known as the district region, called Capernaum (along the Jordan River). Thus, Jesus only passed through the 2ⁿᵈ district of Galilee to reach the 3ʳᵈ district of Galilee, the region of Bethsaida (the way to the sea). Therefore, Jesus never encountered John in Capernaum)

Next, look again at the bold description of the verse below,

John 1:26-28 – ["I baptize with water," John replied, "but among you stands one you do not know. He is the one who comes after me, the straps of whose sandals I am not worthy to untie." **This all happened at Bethany on the other side of the Jordan, where John was baptizing**]

(Note47: This verse as previously revealed is a deceptive trap! The region of Bethany does not represent a region in the land of the eastern hill country, the land of Samaria, nor is it a region in the 2ⁿᵈ district of Galilee, the region called Capernaum. Bethany does not reside near or around the Jordan River. Bethany resides in the land of the western hill country, the land of Jerusalem, which boarders the land of Egypt (Bethany was less than two miles from Jerusalem – John 11:18). Therefore, Jesus was not baptized in a

region of the western hill country, the land of Jerusalem (as referring to Bethany), nor was he baptize in the land of the eastern hill country, the land of Samaria (as referring to Capernaum))

Here is the final revelation: John the Levite never encountered Jesus in the 2nd district of Galilee, nor did he see White Gull birds *(spirits of God)* ascending and descending upon Jesus in the region called Capernaum *(along the Jordan River)*!

{**Important note12:** If you look closely at the description of the verses *'This is the one I meant when I said, 'A man who comes after me has surpassed me because he was before me.' I myself did not know him, but the reason I came baptizing with water was that he might be revealed to Israel'* – John 1:30-31, you will discover that it too, is a deceptive trap! For example, As the revelations has proven, John the Levite never baptize at all *(though he is not called the Baptist)*. Example2: John the Levite grew up in the custom of the Jews and lived in the western hill country, the land of Jerusalem. Jesus grew up in the custom of the Gentiles and lived in the eastern hill country, the land of Samaria *(also known as the land of Israel)*. Therefore, this description *'I came baptizing with water was that he might be revealed to Israel'* is misleading because John was not raised in the eastern hill country, the land of Israel, nor did he frequent the land of Israel as revealed by these two descriptions *'For Jews do not associate with Samaritans* – John 4:9 and *'You are well aware that it is against our law for a Jew to associate with or visit a Gentile'* – Acts 10:28. Therefore, John the Levite never baptize at all, especially in the land of Israel, the eastern hill country, and Jesus did not need to be revealed in the land he is raised, the land of Samaria *(will be called a Nazarene, a Galilean, a Samaritan, and a Gentile)*}

Congratulations! You have successfully revealed the 2nd woe hidden behind the 2nd miraculous sign:

….. **John the Levite never baptized his relative Jesus in the Jordan River within the 2nd district of Galilee, the district region called Capernaum** *(along the Jordan River)*; **but sees white gull birds ascending and descending upon his cousin from the shore region of the 4th district of Galilee** *(the way to the sea)*, **known as the district region called Gennesaret** …..

CHAPTER THREE- 2ND PHASE OF THE CRYPTEX PUZZLE- THE PATH OF THE SIGN

The third and fourth tests in this Chapter is to unveil the mystery revealed behind the [3rd and 4th woes] by revealing the revelation concealed behind the 3rd and 4th miraculous signs: [**Jesus Tempted by the Devil**] and [**The Transfiguration of Jesus**]!

(Note: As revealed in the previous chapter, John the Levite is standing on the Gennesaret Shore region, in the 4th district of Galilee. There are also two other companions that are standing there with him, as he sees his relative Jesus hauling the net of fish into the boats. To reveal the identity of these two natives you must start by looking closely at the following description of Matthew 11:2)

JOHN'S TWO COMPANIONS

The first thing you must do is look closely at the bold portion in the following description of Matthew 11:2-3 below,

> [**When John heard in prison** what Christ was doing, **he sent his disciples** to ask him, "Are you the one who was to come, or should we expect someone else?]

Next, remove the following descriptions from the verses.

1- When John heard in prison
2- he sent his disciples

*(Note2: The following descriptions above reveal two major clues. For example: The following description 'When John heard in prison' corresponds to the capital region city that resides in the 4ᵗʰ district of Galilee. This Capital region represents the city where the palace of king Herod resides (thus, John was beheaded in the city within this region land). This revelation corresponds to the following description '**On hearing this, Pilate asked if the man was a Galilean. When he learned that Jesus was under Herod's jurisdiction, he sent him to Herod**' – Luke 23:6-7. This capital region city will be revealed in more detail moving forward.)*

(Note3: The second clue is the revelation of who the two companions that are standing with John prior to his arrest. For example: The two natives standing on the Gennesaret Shore region (along with John the Levite) does not correspond to any of the names revealed by the twelve disciples. However, one of the names of the twelve disciples holds the clue to revealing exactly who the two companion natives are. To reveal the clues, you must look closely at the following descriptions of Mark 2:14 and Luke 19:2)

Look closely at the bold portion in the two descriptions below,

Mark 2:14 – [As he walked along, **he saw Levi son of Alphaeus sitting at the tax collector's booth**. "Follow me," Jesus told him, and Levi got up and followed him]

Luke 19:2 – [**A man was there by the name of Zacchaeus; he was a chief tax collector** and was wealthy]

To understand where the clues are hidden, you must locate the second clue that reveals them. Look closely at the bolded name in the description below,

Luke 6:13-16 - [When morning came, he called his disciples to him and chose twelve of them, whom he also designated apostles: Simon (whom he named Peter), his brother Andrew, James, John, Philip, Bartholomew, Matthew, Thomas, **James son of Alphaeus**, Simon who was called the Zealot, Judas son of James, and Judas Iscariot, who became a traitor]

*(Note4: If you look closely at this description, **'James son of Alphaeus,'** you will discover the second clue that reveals the first hidden clues. For example: James son of Alphaeus does not represent the brother of Levi son of Alphaeus. Thus, the hidden clue reveals that Levi, the son of Alphaeus, has a brother! The question is what the name of Levi's brother is. The answer to this question reveals where the two hidden clues are located. Example2: The **chief tax collector** is symbolic and corresponds to the word 'elder.' And the **tax collector** is also symbolic and corresponds to the word 'younger.' Example3: The name **(Alphaeus)** is also symbolic and corresponds to these words, **'the father of.'** Thus, Alphaeus represents the father of the chief tax collector and the tax collector))*

Here is the next clue: The next two natives Jesus meets from the region of Bethsaida is the following brothers: [Levi *(younger brother)* and Zacchaeus *(elder brother)*, the sons of Alphaeus]

The next thing you must do is merge the revelations together into the correct context.

- {Nation of Esau} = {Ten Horns} = [Ten kings = Ten tribes: *(Ephraim, Manasseh, Naphtali, Dan, Asher, Issachar, Zebulon, Simeon, Reuben, and Gad)* = Nation of Ephraim = *who are yet to receive a kingdom of their own* = Kingdom of Samaria = Conquered by the Assyrian Empire = Exodus by the Kushite Empire *(Wadi of Egypt)*] = [2nd Exodus] = {Descendants of Esau} = {Eastern hill country} = {Land of Samaria} = {Land of Israel} = {Land of the Gentiles} = [1st District of Galilee = District region of Nazareth *(Joseph, Mary and Jesus exiled)*] = [2nd District of Galilee = District region of Capernaum *(Land of Zebulun and land of Naphtali, the way to the sea, along the Jordan)*] = [3rd District of Galilee = District region of Bethsaida *(Philip, Nathanael, Simon, Andrew, James, John, **Zacchaeus and Levi**)* = Bethsaida Shore region of Galilee] = [4th District of Galilee = District region of Gennesaret = Gennesaret Shore region of Galilee]

- {Nation of Jacob} = {Beast} = [single tribe: *(Benjamin)* = Nation of Judah = *remained in the city* = Conquered by Babylonian Empire = Exodus by the Persian Empire] = [2nd Exodus] = [Kingdom of Jerusalem] = {Descendants of Jacob} = {Western hill country} = {Land of Jerusalem} = {Land of the Jews} = [Hill country of Judea: *(Zechariah, Elizabeth and John son of Zechariah)*] = [Region of Judea: *(Joseph and Mary)*] = [Capital region of Jerusalem = Jerusalem the Holy City: *(John becomes a Levite priest before the Temple courts)*] = [Region of Bethany *(less than two miles from Jerusalem the Holy City)*]

The next thing you must do is look closely at the bold portion in the following description below,

John 1:37-39 - [**When the two disciples heard him say this, they followed Jesus. Turning around, Jesus saw them following and asked, "What do you want?"** They said, "Rabbi" (which means Teacher), **"where are you staying?" "Come," he replied, "and you will see." So they went and saw where he was staying,** and spent that day with him. **It was about the tenth hour**]

Luke 7:20 - [**When the men came to Jesus, they said, "John the Baptist sent us to you** to ask, 'Are you the one who was to come, or should we expect someone else?'

Next, remove the following descriptions from the verses.

1- When the two disciples heard him say this, they followed Jesus
2- Turning around, Jesus saw them following and asked, "What do you want?"
3- "where are you staying?"
4- "Come," he replied, "and you will see"
5- So they went and saw where he was staying
6- It was about the tenth hour
7- When the men came to Jesus, they said, "John the Baptist sent us to you

Next, re-list the following descriptions removed from the verses below,

- "where are you staying?"
- "Come," he replied, "and you will see"
- So they went and saw where he was staying

(Note5: The following descriptions above reveal another major clue. For example: Where is Jesus staying? To reveal the answer to this question you must continue to follow the Path of Jesus as he returns to the 3rd district of Galilee together with his companions. The clue is revealed in the description of Acts 10:5-6. This revelation will be revealed in detail shortly)

Next, re-list the following descriptions removed from the verses below,

- When the two disciples heard him say this, they followed Jesus

(Note6: There is a hidden clue revealed in this description that will reveal how John the Levite arrived in the 4th district of Galilee, on the shore region of Gennesaret, prior to seeing his relative Jesus hauling the nets of fish with his companions in the Sea of Galilee and prior to his arrest. Remember, as previously revealed, John the Levite was not standing on either of the two lands, Zebulun and Naphtali, in the 2nd district of Galilee. Which means, John was not arrested in the region called Capernaum. However, Zacchaeus and Levi were standing with John in the 4th district of Galilee, the shore region called Gennesaret. This means they arrived across the Sea of Galilee somehow. The hidden clue is revealed by James and John, and by Simon and Andrew. For example: The two sets of brothers own their boats and are called fishermen. The hidden clue is Zacchaeus and Levi, the sons of Alphaeus also, own a boat. Therefore, they are not called the tax collectors, they are also called the fishermen. Example2: John the Levite arrived in the Gennesaret shore region in a boat by way of Zacchaeus and Levi the fishermen. Thus, upon John's arrest, Zacchaeus and Levi journeyed across the Sea of Galilee from the Gennesaret shore region and sailed back to the Bethsaida shore region to inform Jesus of John's arrest in the 4th district of Galilee)

{**Important note:** The arrest of John the Levite, apprehended in the 4th district of Galilee, ends the path of John the son of Zechariah. Here, we must return to the Sea of Galilee, the Gennesaret shore limits, where Jesus and his companions are hauling the nets of fish and follow the path of Jesus, as he and his companions return to the 3rd district of Galilee, the region called Bethsaida}

THE PATH OF JESUS

Look closely at the bold portion in the description of Acts 10:5-6 below,

[Now **send men to Joppa** to bring back a man named Simon who is called Peter. **He is staying with Simon the tanner, whose house is by the sea**]

*(Note7: There are two clues revealed in this description. The first clue for example is the name Joppa. The name **'Joppa'** is symbolic and corresponds to the native region of Simon and his brother Andrew. Thus, the biblical city, known as the city of Joppa (by the sea) reveals a paradox that corresponds to the region of Bethsaida, known as the 3rd district of Galilee (the way to the sea))*

*(Note8: The second clue is revealed by the following description 'He is staying with Simon the tanner, whose house is by the sea.' The house of Simon the tanner also reveals a paradox that corresponds to the home of Simon and his brother Andrew. The clue is revealed by the following name: **'tanner!'** For example: There is a paradox revealed by the following two verses, John 1:38 and Acts 10:6 that reveals a hidden clue. For example: If you look closely at this description **'Turning around, Jesus saw them following and asked, "What do you want?" They said, "Rabbi" (which means "Teacher"), "where are you staying?"'** – John 1:38-39, you will discover the answer is revealed by this description **'He is staying with Simon the tanner, whose house is by the sea'** – Acts 10:6. The name 'Simon the tanner' is symbolic and corresponds to the name of Simon and Andrew's father (Thus, they are named after their father's house). This revelation will be revealed in detail shortly. The clue, however, is that the house of Simon the tanner reveals the home of Simon and his brother Andrew. This revelation reveals the meaning behind this description 'they went with James and John to the home of Simon and Andrew' (the house of Tanner) - Mark 1:29 (whose house is by the sea of Galilee))*

Here is the next clue: Jesus is staying at the home of the following natives of Bethsaida: [Simon and Andrew, the sons of Tanner].

The next thing you must do is look closely at the bold portion in the following descriptions below,

Luke 4:38-39 'Jesus left the synagogue and went to the home of Simon. Now **Simon's mother in-law was suffering from a high fever, and they asked Jesus to help her.** So he bent over her and rebuked the fever, and it left her. She got up at once and began to wait on them."

Mark 1:29-31 'As soon as they left the synagogue, they went with James and John to the home of Simon and Andrew. **Simon's mother-in-law was in bed with a fever, and they told Jesus about her.** So he went to her, took her hand and helped her up. The fever left her and she began to wait on them."

Next, remove the next following description from the verses.

- Simon's mother in-law was suffering from a high fever, and they asked Jesus to help her
- Simon's mother-in-law was in bed with a fever, and they told Jesus about her

*(Note9: These two descriptions also reveal another major clue. For example: The following description 'Simon's mother in-law' is written deceptively. Example2: Simon's mother-in-law reveals another paradox that corresponds to the name 'Tanner.' This revelation also corresponds to this description '**He is staying with Simon the tanner, whose house is by the sea.**' Simon's mother-in-law is symbolic and corresponds to Simon and Andrew's biological mother (a widowed wife). Thus, she corresponds to the house of Tanner (whose house is by the sea) and represents the widowed wife of Simon the tanner (the way to the sea). Therefore, Simon was never married! This revelation corresponds to the bold portion of this description '**send men to Joppa to bring back a man named Simon** who is called Peter' (Thus, Simon is not called Peter, but is called 'the son of Tanner'). As revealed previously, the name Joppa represents a city that is near the sea and corresponds to the 3rd district of Galilee, known as the region of Bethsaida. Therefore, the house of tanner (whose house is by the sea in the city of Joppa) corresponds to the home of Simon and Andrew, the sons of Tanner (whose house is by the sea in the region of Bethsaida))*

{**Important note2:** There are three sets of brothers that are fishermen and named after their father's house in their native region of Bethsaida. The three brothers are as follows: **James and John, the sons of Zebedee, Simon and Andrew, the sons of Tanner**, and **Zacchaeus and Levi, the sons of Alphaeus**}

The next thing you must do is re-list the entire descriptions removed from the verses and place the bold descriptions in the correct number order according to the context of the story.

[25] **When the two disciples heard him say this, they followed Jesus**

[26] **Turning around, Jesus saw them following** and asked, "What do you want?"

[29] **"where are you staying?"**

[30] **"Come," he replied, "and you will see"**

[31] **So they went and saw where he was staying**

[32] **It was about the tenth hour**

[27] **When the men came to Jesus, they said, "John** the Baptist [28] **sent us to you**

Next, remove the bold descriptions in numbered order and reconstruct them into the correct context of the story as seen below,

[25] When the two disciples heard him say this, they followed Jesus [26] Turning around, Jesus saw them following [27] When the men came to Jesus, they said, "John [28] sent us to you [29] "where are you staying?" [30] "Come," he replied, "and you will see" [31] So they went and saw where he was staying [32] It was about the tenth hour

To reveal the sixth piece to the sacred document of Immanuel you must merge the revelations into the correct context as seen below,

[Leaving Nazareth *(1st district of Galilee)*, he went in Capernaum *(2nd district of Galilee)* Land of Zebulun and land of Naphtali, the way to the sea *(Sea of Galilee)*, along the Jordan *(Jordan River)*] [The next day Jesus decided to leave for the town of Bethsaida *(3rd district of Galilee)*] [Now Philip was from Bethsaida, Philip found Nathanael and told him -Jesus of Nazareth, the son of Joseph."][As Jesus walked beside the Sea of Galilee, *(accompanied by Philip and Nathanael)* he saw at the water's edge *(Bethsaida shore region)* two boats, left there by the fishermen *(companions of Philip and Nathanael)*. He saw two brothers - Simon and his brother Andrew, who were washing their nets and asked him to put out a little from shore *(sail beyond the Bethsaida shore region limit)*. He got into one of the boats, the one belonging to Simon *(accompanied by Andrew, Philip and Nathanael)*. Put out into deep water and let down the nets for a catch *(sail to the Gennesaret shore region)*][When he *(Simon)* had gone a little farther, he saw two other brothers, James's son of Zebedee and his brother John *(fishing companions)* in a boat, preparing their nets. Going on from there, *(crossing the Bethsaida border into the Gennesaret region)* his companions *(Simon, Andrew, Philip and Nathanael)* were astonished at the catch of fish they had taken, and so were James and John, the sons of Zebedee *(native companions from the Bethsaida region)* Simon's partners.' So they signaled their partners in the other boat *(James and John -sons of Zebedee)* to come and help them, and they came *(from Bethsaida shore region)* and filled both boats so full that they began to sink *(Gennesaret shore region)*][**When the two disciples *(Zacchaeus and Levi the sons of Alphaeus)* heard him say this, they followed Jesus *(returned to Bethsaida)*. Turning around, Jesus saw them following. When the men came to Jesus, they said, "John *(your relative)* sent us to you "where are you staying?" "Come," he replied, "and you will see". So they went and saw where he was staying *(home of Simon and Andrew, the sons of Tanner)*. It was about the tenth hour**]

(Note10: The following description 'it was about the tenth hour' is also symbolic and reveals another major clue. This revelation will be revealed in detail momentarily)

The next thing you must do is look closely at the bold portion in the following descriptions below,

Mark 1:32 - [**That evening after sunset** the people brought to Jesus all the sick and demon possessed]

Mark 4:35-36 - [**That day when evening came**, he said to his disciples, **"Let us go over to the other side.** Leaving the crowd behind, they took him along, just as he was, **in the boat]**

John 6:16-17 - [**When evening came**, his disciples **went down to the lake**, **where they got into a boat and set off across the lake for** Capernaum]

Luke 4:40 - [**When the sun was setting**, the people brought to Jesus all who had various kinds of sickness, and laying his hands on each one, he healed them]

Luke 4:42 - [At daybreak **Jesus went out to a solitary place.** The people were looking for him and when they came to where he was, they tried to keep him from leaving them]

Matthew 8:16 - [**When evening came**, many who were demon-possessed were brought to him, and he drove out the spirits with a word and healed all the sick]

Matthew 13:1-2 - [**That same day Jesus went out of the house and sat by the lake.** Such large crowds gathered around him that **he got into a boat** and sat in it, while all the people stood on the shore]

Matthew 15:29 - [**Jesus left there and went along the Sea of Galilee]**

Matthew 4:12 - [**When Jesus heard that John had been put in prison, he returned to Galilee]**

Next, remove the following descriptions from the verses.

1- That evening after sunset

2- That day when evening came

3- Let us go over to the other side in the boat

4- When evening came

5- went down to the lake, where they got into a boat

6- set off across the lake for

7- When the sun was setting

8- Jesus went out to a solitary place

9- When evening came

10- That same day Jesus went out of the house and sat by the lake

11- he got into a boat

12- went along the Sea of Galilee

13- When Jesus heard that John had been put in prison, he returned to Galilee

Next, re-list the following descriptions removed from the verses.

- [That evening after sunset]
- [That day when evening came]
- [When evening came]
- [When the sun was setting]

(Note11: These descriptions above reveal a hidden clue. For example: The late evening corresponds to the setting of the Sun (sunset). Thus, the late evening (sunset) corresponds to the description 'It was about the tenth hour' and represent the following time of day: 10:00 p.m. (sunset))

Next, re-list the following description removed from the verses.

- [When Jesus heard that John had been put in prison, he returned to Galilee]

*(Note12: This description reveals another hidden clue. For example: Zacchaeus and Levi the sons of Alphaeus inform Jesus of John's arrest in the 4th district of Galilee, along the Gennesaret shore region (where John saw his relative hauling the net of fish). This revelation corresponds to the following description 'Which way did he go?" And his sons showed him which road the man of God from Judah had taken' – 1st Kings 13:12. Thus, the description '**Which way did he go**' is symbolic and corresponds to the 4th district of Galilee, the region of Gennesaret where John was arrested. This region will be revealed in more detail moving forward. This description '**And his sons showed him**' is symbolic and corresponds to the sons of Alphaeus (Zacchaeus and Levi). This description '**showed him which road**' is symbolic and corresponds to the following place, the northeast region of the Valley of Sychar. This region will also be revealed in more detail moving forward. This description '**the man of God from Judah had taken**' is symbolic and corresponds to John the Levite (the only descendant of Aaron who exiled himself from the western hill country, the land of the Jews (the descendants of Judah). The final description '**he returned to Galilee**' corresponds to the shore region where Jesus and his companions were hauling the nets of fish (The 4th district of Galilee). This revelation will be revealed in more detail shortly))*

Next, re-list the following descriptions removed from the verses.

- [went down to the lake, where they got into a boat]
- [Jesus went out to a solitary place]
- [That same day Jesus went out of the house and sat by the lake]
- [he got into a boat]
- [went along the Sea of Galilee]

(Note13: The following descriptions above also reveal another hidden clue. For example: These descriptions 'That same day Jesus went out of the house' and 'went along the Sea of Galilee' as well as 'where they got into a boat' corresponds to this description 'Jesus went out to a solitary place.' The solitary place is symbolic and corresponds to the following two descriptions 'Put out into deep water and let down the nets for a catch' – Luke 5:4, and 'That day when evening came, he said to his disciples, "Let us go over to the other side' – Mark 4:35. This revelation will be revealed in more detail shortly)

96

Next, re-list the following descriptions removed from the verses.

- [Let us go over to the other side in the boat]
- [set off across the lake for]
- [When Jesus heard that John had been put in prison, he returned to Galilee]

(Note14: The following descriptions above also reveals another hidden clue. For example: The other side of the Sea of Galilee represents the 4ᵗʰ district of Galilee. Thus, the descriptions 'Let us go over to the other side' and 'set off across' corresponds to the district shore region of Gennesaret. This revelation reveals the meaning behind this description 'he returned to Galilee' (4ᵗʰ district of Galilee, the region called Gennesaret). Thus, this description 'Jesus went out to a solitary place' corresponds to this description 'he returned to Galilee'. This revelation will also be revealed in more detail shortly))

The next thing you must do is re-list the entire descriptions removed from the verses and place the bold descriptions in the correct number order according to the context of the story.

That evening after sunset

[33] **That day when evening came**

[37] **Let us go over to the other side** in [38] **the boat**

When evening came

went down to the lake, where [40] **they got into a boat**

[41] **set off across the** lake for Capernaum

[34] **When the sun was setting**

At daybreak

Jesus went out [44] **to a solitary place**

When evening came

[39] **That same day** Jesus [36] **went out of the house** and sat by the lake

he got into a boat

went along the [42] **Sea of Galilee**

[35] **When Jesus heard that John had been put in prison, he** [43] **returned to Galilee**

Next, remove the descriptions in the numbered order and construct them into the correct context as seen below,

[33] That day when evening came [34] When the sun was setting [35] 'When Jesus heard that John had been put in prison [36] he went out of the house [37] "Let us go over to the other side" [38] That same day [39] they got into [40] the boat [41] set off across the [42] Sea of Galilee, [43] returned to Galilee [44] to a solitary place

To reveal the seventh piece to the sacred document of Immanuel you must merge the revelations into the correct context as seen below,

[Leaving Nazareth *(1ˢᵗ district of Galilee)*, he went in Capernaum *(2ⁿᵈ district of Galilee)* Land of Zebulun and land of Naphtali, the way to the sea *(Sea of Galilee)*, along the Jordan *(Jordan River)*] [The next day Jesus decided to leave for the town of Bethsaida *(3ʳᵈ district of Galilee)*] [Now Philip was from Bethsaida, Philip found Nathanael and told him -Jesus of Nazareth, the son of Joseph."][As Jesus walked beside the Sea of Galilee, *(accompanied by Philip and Nathanael)* he saw at the water's edge *(Bethsaida shore region)* two boats, left there by the fishermen *(companions of Philip and Nathanael)*. He saw two brothers - Simon and his brother Andrew, who were washing their nets and asked him to put out a little from shore *(sail beyond the Bethsaida shore region limit)*. He got into one of the boats, the one belonging to Simon *(accompanied by Andrew, Philip and Nathanael)*. Put out into deep water and let down the nets for a catch *(sail to the Gennesaret shore region)*][When he *(Simon)* had gone a little farther, he saw two other brothers, James's son of Zebedee and his brother John *(fishing companions)* in a boat, preparing their nets. Going on from there, *(crossing the Bethsaida border into the Gennesaret region)* his companions *(Simon, Andrew, Philip and Nathanael)* were astonished at the catch of fish they had taken, and so were James and John, the sons of Zebedee *(native companions from the Bethsaida region)* Simon's partners.' So they signaled their partners in the other boat *(James and John -sons of Zebedee)* to come and help them, and they came *(from Bethsaida shore region)* and filled both boats so full that they began to sink *(Gennesaret shore region)*][When the two disciples *(Zacchaeus and Levi the sons of Alphaeus)* heard him say this, they followed Jesus *(returned to Bethsaida)*. Turning around, Jesus saw them following. When the men came to Jesus, they said, "John *(your relative)* sent us to you "where are you staying?" "Come," he replied, "and you will see". So they went and saw where he was staying *(home of Simon and Andrew, the sons of Tanner)*. It was about the tenth hour][**That day when**

98

evening came *(10:00 p.m.)*, When the sun was setting *(sunset)*, 'When Jesus heard that John had been put in prison he went out of the house *(home of Simon and Andrew the sons of Tanner)*. "Let us go over to the other side" *(Gennesaret shore region)*. That same day they got into the boat set off across the Sea of Galilee, returned to Galilee *(4th district of Galilee)* to a solitary place]

The next thing you must do is look closely at the bold portion in the following descriptions below,

Mark 4:35-36 - [That day when evening came, he said to his disciples, "Let us go over to the other side. Leaving the crowd behind, **they took him along, just as he was, in the boat**]

Mark 1:38-39 - [Jesus replied, **"Let us go somewhere else to the nearby villages,** so I can preach there also. So he traveled throughout Galilee, preaching in their synagogues and driving out demons]

Mark 5:1-2 - [**They went across the lake to the region of the Gerasenes.** When Jesus got out of the boat, a man with an impure spirit came from the tombs to meet him]

Mark 6:32-33 - [**So they went away by themselves in a boat to a solitary place.** But many who saw them leaving recognized them and ran on foot from all the towns and got there ahead of them]

Mark 7:33 - [**When they had crossed over, they landed at Gennesaret and anchored there**]

Matthew 8:28 - [**When he arrived at the other side in the region of the Gadarenes,** two demon-possessed men coming from the tombs met him]

Matthew 14:34 - [**When they had crossed over, they landed at Gennasaret**]

Matthew 15:21 - [**Leaving that place, Jesus withdrew to the region of Tyre and Sidon**]

Matthew 16:5 - [**When they went across the lake,** the disciples forgot to take bread]

Matthew 16:13 - [**When Jesus came to the region of Caesarea Philippi,** he asked his disciples, "Who do people say the Son of Man is?]

Luke 8:22 - [One day Jesus said to his disciples, **"Let's go over to the other side of the lake." So they got into a boat and set out**]

Luke 8:26-27 - [**They sailed to the region of the Gerasenes, which is across the lake from Galilee. When Jesus stepped ashore,** he was met by a demon-possessed man from the town]

John 6:1-2 - **[Sometime after this, Jesus crossed to the far shore of the Sea of Galilee (that is, the Sea of Tiberias)**, and a great crowed of people followed him because they saw the miraculous signs he had performed on the sick]

Next, remove the following descriptions from the verses.

1- "Let us go over to the other side, they took him along, just as he was, in the boat

2- Let us go somewhere else to the nearby villages

3- They went across the lake to the region of the Gerasenes

4- So they went away by themselves in a boat to a solitary place

5- When they had crossed over, they landed at Gennesaret and anchored there

6- When he arrived at the other side in the region of the Gadarenes,

7- When they had crossed over, they landed at Gennasaret

8- Leaving that place, Jesus withdrew to the region of Tyre and Sidon

9- When they went across the lake

10- When Jesus came to the region of Caesarea Philippi

11- "Let's go over to the other side of the lake." So they got into a boat and set out.'"

12- They sailed to the region of the Gerasenes, which is across the lake from Galilee. When Jesus stepped ashore

13- Sometime after this, Jesus crossed to the far shore of the Sea of Galilee (that is, the Sea of Tiberias)

Next, re-list the following description removed from the verses.

- [Sometime after this, Jesus crossed to the far shore of the Sea of Galilee (that is, the Sea of Tiberias)]

- [When Jesus came to the region of Caesarea Philippi]

(Note15: These descriptions reveal another hidden clue. For example: The Sea of Tiberias is symbolic and corresponds to this description 'Let us go over to the other side.' Thus, the 'other side' represents the Gennesaret shore region (where Jesus and his companions were hauling the nets of fish). Therefore, the Sea of Tiberias corresponds to the Sea of Galilee (shore region of Gennesaret). The region Caesarea Philippi is also symbolic and corresponds to one of the regions that make-up the 4th district of Galilee, (thus, the 4th district called Gennesaret consist of two region lands). This particular region is not called Caesarea Philippi though it is written Caesarea Philippi. There is another region name that will reveal the name of the true region (Thus, Caesarea Philippi is a deceptive trap). The true name of this region land will be revealed momentarily!))

Next, re-list the following description removed from the verses.

- [They went across the lake to the region of the Gerasenes]
- [They sailed to the region of the Gerasenes, which is across the lake from Galilee. When Jesus stepped ashore]

(Note16: The following descriptions above is written deceptively and contains another hidden clue. For example: The 4ᵗʰ district of Galilee is divided into two regions (one of the regions represents the region of the Gerasenes). The other region is hidden behind the understanding of this description 'Jesus withdrew to the region of Tyre and Sidon.')

*(Note17: The region of Tyre and Sidon is symbolic and corresponds to the coast of Tyre and the coast of Sidon. This revelation corresponds to the bold portion of this description 'A large crowd of his disciples was there and a great number of people from all over Judea, from Jerusalem, **and from the coastal region around Tyre and Sidon**' – Luke 6:17 (Thus, the two coastal regions does not correspond to the land of the western hill country, the land of Jerusalem). The coast of Sidon and the coast of Tyre represent two coastal regions that make up the 4ᵗʰ district of Galilee (the eastern hill country, the land of Samaria). For example: The 'coast of Sidon' corresponds to the northeast region of the valley of Sychar, the region of the Gerasenes. The 'coast of Tyre' corresponds to the southwest region of the valley of Sychar, the region of the Gadarenes. Thus, the region of Caesarea Philippi is symbolic and corresponds to the following description **'he arrived at the other side in the region of the Gadarenes'** – Matthew 8:28. Therefore, the following two descriptions 'They went across the lake to the region of the Gerasenes' and 'They sailed to the region of the Gerasenes, which is across the lake from Galilee' are both deceptive traps because the region of the Gerasenes (northeast region of the valley of Sychar) is not located near the Sea of Galilee. On the contrary, the region of the Gerasenes is in the desert hill region land (coast of Sidon). This revelation will be revealed in more detail moving forward. The region of the Gadarenes also corresponds to this description **'they went away by themselves in a boat to a solitary place'** - Mark 6:32-33. This region of land (across the Sea of Galilee) is also known as a remote region land (accessible by crossing the Sea of Galilee by boat). The region of the Gerasenes and the region of the Gadarenes as well as the coastal regions of Tyre and Sidon will be revealed in more detail moving forward and throughout the 3ʳᵈ Chronicle series of the Elijah Doctrine))*

The next thing you must do is merge the revelations together into the correct context.

- {Nation of Esau} = {Ten Horns} = [Ten kings = Ten tribes: *(Ephraim, Manasseh, Naphtali, Dan, Asher, Issachar, Zebulon, Simeon, Reuben, and Gad)* = Nation of Ephraim = *who are yet to receive a kingdom of their own* = Kingdom of Samaria = Conquered by the Assyrian Empire = Exodus by the Kushite Empire *(Wadi of Egypt)*] = [2nd Exodus] = {Descendants of Esau} = {Eastern hill country} = {Land of Samaria} = {Land of Israel} = {Land of the Gentiles} = [1st District of Galilee = District region of Nazareth *(Joseph, Mary and Jesus exiled)*] = [2nd District of Galilee = District region of Capernaum *(Land of Zebulun and land of Naphtali, the way to the sea, along the Jordan)*] = [3rd District of Galilee = District region of Bethsaida *(Philip, Nathanael, Simon, Andrew, James, John, Zacchaeus and Levi)* = Bethsaida Shore region of Galilee] = [4th District of Galilee = District region of Gennesaret **(coast of Tyre and Sidon)** = Gennesaret Shore region of Galilee **(Sea of Tiberias)**] = **[Region of the Gadarenes *(Caesarea Philippi)* = Region of the Gerasenes]**

- {Nation of Jacob} = {Beast} = [single tribe: *(Benjamin)* = Nation of Judah = *remained in the city* = Conquered by Babylonian Empire = Exodus by the Persian Empire] = [2nd Exodus] = [Kingdom of Jerusalem] = {Descendants of Jacob} = {Western hill country} = {Land of Jerusalem} = {Land of the Jews} = [Hill country of Judea: *(Zechariah, Elizabeth and John son of Zechariah)*] = [Region of Judea: *(Joseph and Mary)*] = [Capital region of Jerusalem = Jerusalem the Holy City: *(John becomes a Levite priest before the Temple courts)*] = [Region of Bethany *(less than two miles from Jerusalem the Holy City)*]

The next thing you must do is re-list the entire descriptions removed from the verses and place the bold descriptions in the correct number order according to the context of the story.

"Let us go over to the other side, they took him along, just as he was, in the boat

Let us go somewhere else to the nearby villages

They went across the lake to the region of the Gerasenes

So they went away by themselves in a boat to a solitary place

When they had crossed over, [47] **they landed at Gennesaret and anchored there**

[46] **When he arrived at the other side in the region of the Gadarenes**,

When they had crossed over, they landed at Gennasaret

Leaving that place, Jesus withdrew to the region of Tyre and Sidon

When they went across the lake

When Jesus came to the region of Caesarea Philippi

"Let's go over to the other side of the lake." So they got into a boat and set out.'"

They sailed to the region of the Gerasenes, which is across the lake from Galilee. [48] **When Jesus stepped ashore**

Sometime after this, [45] **Jesus crossed to the far shore of the Sea of Galilee** (that is, the Sea of Tiberias)

Next, remove the descriptions in the numbered order and reconstruct them into the correct context as seen below,

[45] Jesus crossed to the far shore of the Sea of Galilee **[46]** When he arrived at the other side in the region of the Gadarenes, **[47]** they landed at Gennesaret and anchored there **[48]** When Jesus stepped ashore

To reveal the eighth piece to the sacred document of Immanuel you must merge the revelations into the correct context as seen below,

[Leaving Nazareth *(1st district of Galilee)*, he went in Capernaum *(2nd district of Galilee)* Land of Zebulun and land of Naphtali, the way to the sea *(Sea of Galilee)*, along the Jordan *(Jordan River)*] [The next day Jesus decided to leave for the town of Bethsaida *(3rd district of Galilee)*] [Now Philip was from Bethsaida, Philip found Nathanael and told him -Jesus of Nazareth, the son of Joseph."][As Jesus walked beside the Sea of Galilee, *(accompanied by Philip and Nathanael)* he saw at the water's edge *(Bethsaida shore region)* two boats, left there by the fishermen *(companions of Philip and Nathanael)*. He saw two brothers - Simon and his brother Andrew, who were washing their nets and asked him to put out a little from shore *(sail beyond the Bethsaida shore region limit)*. He got into one of the boats, the one belonging to Simon *(accompanied by Andrew, Philip and Nathanael)*. Put out into deep water and let down the nets for a catch *(sail to the Gennesaret shore region)*][When he *(Simon)* had gone a little farther, he saw two other brothers, James's son of Zebedee and his brother John *(fishing companions)* in a boat, preparing their nets. Going on from there, *(crossing the Bethsaida border into the Gennesaret region)* his companions *(Simon, Andrew, Philip and Nathanael)* were astonished at the catch of fish they had taken, and so were James and John, the sons of Zebedee *(native companions from the Bethsaida region)* Simon's partners.' So they signaled their partners in the other boat *(James and John -sons of Zebedee)* to come and help them, and they came *(from Bethsaida shore region)* and filled both boats so full that they began to sink *(Gennesaret shore region)*][When the two disciples *(Zacchaeus and Levi the sons of Alphaeus)* heard him say this, they followed Jesus *(returned to Bethsaida)*. Turning around, Jesus saw them following. When the men came to Jesus, they said, "John *(your relative)* sent us to you "where are you staying?" "Come," he replied, "and you will see". So they went and saw where he was staying *(home of Simon and Andrew, the sons of Tanner)*. It was about the tenth hour][That day when evening came *(10:00 p.m.)*, When the sun was setting *(sunset)*, 'When Jesus heard that John had been put in prison he went out of the house *(home of Simon and Andrew the sons of Tanner)*. "Let us go over to the other side" *(Gennesaret shore region)*. That same day they got into the boat set off across the Sea of Galilee, returned to Galilee *(4th district of Galilee)* to a solitary place]**[Jesus crossed to the far shore of the Sea of Galilee. When he arrived at the other side in the region of the Gadarenes, they landed at Gennesaret and anchored there** *(boats of Simon and Andrew, and James and John)*. **When Jesus stepped ashore]**

The next thing you must do is look closely at the bold portion in the following descriptions below,

Luke 8:27 - [**When Jesus stepped ashore, he was met by a demon-possessed man from the town**]

Mark 5:2 - [**When Jesus got out of the boat, a man with an impure spirit** came from the tombs **to meet him**]

Matthew 8:28 - [**When he arrived at the other side in the region of the Gadarenes, two demon-possessed men** coming from the tombs **met him**]

Next, remove the following descriptions from the verses.

1- When Jesus stepped ashore
2- he was met by a demon-possessed man from the town
3- When Jesus got out of the boat
4- a man with an impure spirit came to meet him
5- When he arrived at the other side in the region of the Gadarenes
6- two demon-possessed men met him

Next, re-list the following descriptions removed from the verses.

- he was met by a demon-possessed man from the town
- a man with an impure came to meet him

*(Note18: The following two descriptions above reveal a vital clue. For example: The man with the **impure spirit** (who met him) is symbolic and corresponds to the **demon-possessed** man from the town. Thus, to uncover his true identity you must begin by separating the two symbolic descriptions that describes the man from the town)*

Look closely at the following descriptions as seen below,

- [a man with an impure spirit came to meet him] = [?]
- [he was met by a demon-possessed man] = [?]

(Note19: To reveal the mystery name hidden behind the descriptions above you must locate another clue revealed in the descriptions of Luke 22:3, John 13:27, Mark 5:9 and Luke 8:30))

Look closely at the bold portion in the following four descriptions below,

1- Luke 22:3 – [Then **Satan entered Judas, called Iscariot**, one of the Twelve]

2- John 13:27 – [As soon as Judas took the bread, **Satan entered into him**]

3- Mark 5:9 – [Then Jesus asked him, "What is your name?" **"My name is Legion," he replied, "for we are many**]

4- Luke 8:30 – [Jesus asked him, "What is your name?" **"Legion," he replied, because many demons had gone into him**]

Next, remove only the bold descriptions from the verses.

- [Satan entered Judas, called Iscariot]
- [Satan entered into him]
- ["My name is Legion," he replied, "for we are many]
- ["Legion," he replied, because many demons had gone into him]

*(Note20: The following two descriptions '**Satan entered Judas**' and '**Satan entered into him**' are symbolic and corresponds to this description '**a man with an impure spirit**' - Mark 5:2. This revelation corresponds to this description "I have sinned," he said, "**for I have betrayed innocent blood.**" - Matthew 27:5. Thus, the man with an impure spirit corresponds to the name '**Iscariot.**' This revelation will be revealed in detail shortly))*

*(Note21: The following two descriptions '"**My name is Legion," he replied, "for we are many'** and '"**Legion," he replied, because many demons had gone into him'** are symbolic and corresponds to this description '**demon possessed man.'** This revelation corresponds to this description '**the man who had been possessed by the legion of demons'** – Mark 5:15. Thus, the demon-possessed man corresponds to the name '**Legion.'** This revelation will be revealed in detail shortly))*

Next, merge the following two names together in the proper context.

- {a man with an impure spirit came to meet him} = [Satan entered Judas] = **[Iscariot]**
- {he was met by a demon-possessed man} = [many demons had gone into him] = **[Legion]**

*(Note22: The following two names 'Legion' and 'Iscariot' are symbolic and corresponds to the description '**two demon possessed men coming from the tomb met him'** – Matthew 8:28.' To illustrate this, look closely at the following example below)*

Look closely at the illustration regarding the previous full descriptions merged into the correct context as seen below,

- **1st demon-possessed man** = [a man with an impure spirit came to meet him = Satan entered Judas = Iscariot]

- **2nd demon-possessed man** = [he was met by a demon-possessed man = many demons had gone into him = Legion]

Here is the next clue: The following two descriptions '**demon-possessed man from the town (Legion)'** and '**a man with an impure spirit (Iscariot)'** corresponds to the description 'two demon-possessed men coming from the tomb met him' and represents the name of a native who resides in the region of the Gadarenes: [Judas the Gadarene].

The next thing you must do is merge the revelations together into the correct context.

- {Nation of Esau} = {Ten Horns} = [Ten kings = Ten tribes: *(Ephraim, Manasseh, Naphtali, Dan, Asher, Issachar, Zebulon, Simeon, Reuben, and Gad)* = Nation of Ephraim = *who are yet to receive a kingdom of their own* = Kingdom of Samaria = Conquered by the Assyrian Empire = Exodus by the Kushite Empire *(Wadi of Egypt)*] = [2nd Exodus] = {Descendants of Esau} = {Eastern hill country} = {Land of Samaria} = {Land of Israel} = {Land of the Gentiles} = [1st District of Galilee = District region of Nazareth *(Joseph, Mary and Jesus exiled)*] = [2nd District of Galilee = District region of Capernaum *(Land of Zebulun and land of Naphtali, the way to the sea, along the Jordan)*] = [3rd District of Galilee = District region of Bethsaida *(Philip, Nathanael, Simon, Andrew, James, John, Zacchaeus and Levi)* = Bethsaida Shore region of Galilee] = [4th District of Galilee = District region of Gennesaret *(coast of Tyre and Sidon)* = Gennesaret Shore region of Galilee *(Sea of Tiberias)*] = [Region of the Gadarenes *(Caesarea Philippi)* = **(Judas the Gadarene)**] = [Region of the Gerasenes]

- {Nation of Jacob} = {Beast} = [single tribe: *(Benjamin)* = Nation of Judah = *remained in the city* = Conquered by Babylonian Empire = Exodus by the Persian Empire] = [2nd Exodus] = [Kingdom of Jerusalem] = {Descendants of Jacob} = {Western hill country} = {Land of Jerusalem} = {Land of the Jews} = [Hill country of Judea: *(Zechariah, Elizabeth and John son of Zechariah)*] = [Region of Judea: *(Joseph and Mary)*] = [Capital region of Jerusalem = Jerusalem the Holy City: *(John becomes a Levite priest before the Temple courts)*] = [Region of Bethany *(less than two miles from Jerusalem the Holy City)*]

{**Important note3:** If you look closely at this description, *'When Jesus landed and saw a large crowd, he had compassion on them and healed their sick.'* – Matthew 14:14, you will discover it too, is a deceptive trap! For example: When the two boats landed in the district region called Gennesaret, Jesus was meant by one man from the region of the Gadarenes, Judas the Gadarene *(was not meant by a large crowd)*. Thus, Jesus and his companions arrived and landed in the region of the Gadarenes, from the shore region of Gennesaret}

{**Important note4:** If you look closely at this description, *'As evening approached, the disciples came to him and said, "This is a remote place, and it's already getting late. Send the crowds away, so they can go to the villages and buy themselves some food.'* – Matthew 14:15, you will discover it too, is a deceptive trap! For example: The following description *'This is a remote place'* is symbolic and corresponds to this description *'he arrived at the other side in the region of the Gadarenes'* – Matthew 8:28. Thus, the region of the Gadarenes can only be reached by boat *(crossing the Sea of Galilee)*. This revelation also corresponds to the following two descriptions **'*Put out into deep water* and let down the nets for a catch'** *(shore region of Gennesaret)* – Luke 5:4, and **'*Let us go over to the other side*'** *(4th district of Galilee)* – Mark 4:35. Therefore, this description *'This is a remote place'* corresponds to this description *'Jesus went out to a solitary place'* – Luke 4:42. Example2: This description *'and it's already getting late'* is also symbolic and corresponds to the time of day Jesus and his companions arrive in the 4th district of Galilee, to the region of the Gadarenes. The time the two boats arrive is 11:00 p.m. (late evening). This revelation corresponds to this description **'*That day when evening came (10:00 p.m.), he said to his disciples, "Let us go over to the other side'*** *(arrived in the region of the Gadarenes at 11:00 p.m.)* – Mark 4:35}

{**Important note5:** If you look closely at the descriptions of the verses, **'*Jesus replied, "They do not need to go away. You give them something to eat." "We have here only five loaves of bread and two fish," they answered. Bring them here to me," he said. And he directed the people to sit down on the grass. Taking the five loaves and the two fish and looking up to heaven, he gave thanks and broke the loaves. Then he gave them to the disciples and the disciples gave them to the people. They all ate and were satisfied, and the disciples picked up twelve basketfuls of broken pieces that were left over. The number of those who ate was about five thousand men, besides women and children'*** – Matthew 14:16-21, you will discover it too, is a deceptive trap! Jesus and his companions were meant by one native in the region of the Gadarenes at 11:00 p.m. when he stepped ashore. Therefore, Jesus never fed a crowd in this remote region, the region of the Gadarenes, at the 11th hour (late evening). On the contrary, the trap is revealed by this description *'Put out into deep water and let down the nets for a catch'* – Luke 5:4. For example: The boats of Simon and Andrew, the sons of Tanner, and James and John, the sons of Zebedee, sailed beyond the border limits of the Bethsaida shore region, and filled their boats full of fish from the shore region of Gennesaret and returned to the shore region of Bethsaida *(where they unloaded the nets of fish from the boats)*, prior to returning again to the shore region of Gennesaret *(no nets of fish aboard the boats)*. This revelation corresponds to the following two descriptions *'Let's go over to the other side of the lake." So they got into a boat and set out'* – Luke 8:22 and *'When Jesus stepped ashore, he was met by a demon-possessed man from the town'* – Luke 8:27. Thus, revealing the meaning behind this description *'he arrived at the other side in the region of the Gadarenes'* – Matthew 8:28. Therefore, Jesus met Judas the Gadarene in the late evening of day *(he never met a crowd)*}

The next thing you must do is re-list the entire descriptions removed from the verses and place the bold descriptions in the correct number order according to the context of the story.

When Jesus stepped ashore

[51] **he was met by a demon-possessed man from the town**

When [49] **Jesus got out of the boat**

[50] **a man with an impure spirit to came meet him**

When he arrived at the other side in the region of the Gadarenes

two demon-possessed men met him

Next, remove the descriptions in the numbered order and reconstruct them into the correct context as seen below,

[49] Jesus got out of the boat [50] a man with an impure spirit came to meet him [51] he was met by a demon-possessed man from the town

To reveal the ninth piece to the sacred document of Immanuel you must merge the revelations into the correct context as seen below,

[Leaving Nazareth *(1st district of Galilee)*, he went in Capernaum *(2nd district of Galilee)* Land of Zebulun and land of Naphtali, the way to the sea *(Sea of Galilee)*, along the Jordan *(Jordan River)*] [The next day Jesus decided to leave for the town of Bethsaida *(3rd district of Galilee)*] [Now Philip was from Bethsaida, Philip found Nathanael and told him -Jesus of Nazareth, the son of Joseph."][As Jesus walked beside the Sea of Galilee, *(accompanied by Philip and Nathanael)* he saw at the water's edge *(Bethsaida shore region)* two boats, left there by the fishermen *(companions of Philip and Nathanael)*. He saw two brothers - Simon and his brother Andrew, who were washing their nets and asked him to put out a little from shore *(sail beyond the Bethsaida shore region limit)*. He got into one of the boats, the one belonging to Simon *(accompanied by Andrew, Philip and Nathanael)*. Put out into deep water and let down the nets for a catch *(sail to the Gennesaret shore region)*][When he *(Simon)* had gone a little farther, he saw two other brothers, James's son of Zebedee and his brother John *(fishing companions)* in a boat, preparing their nets. Going on from there, *(crossing the Bethsaida border into the Gennesaret region)* his companions *(Simon, Andrew, Philip and Nathanael)* were astonished at the catch of fish they had taken, and so were James and John, the sons of Zebedee *(native companions from the Bethsaida region)* Simon's partners.' So they signaled their partners in the other boat *(James and John -sons of Zebedee)* to come and help them, and they came *(from Bethsaida shore region)* and filled both boats so full that they began to sink *(Gennesaret shore region)*][When the two disciples *(Zacchaeus and Levi the sons of Alphaeus)* heard him say this, they followed Jesus *(returned to Bethsaida)*. Turning around, Jesus saw them following. When the men came to Jesus, they said, "John *(your relative)* sent us to you "where are you staying?" "Come," he replied, "and you will see". So they went and saw where he was staying *(home of Simon and Andrew, the sons of Tanner)*. It was about the tenth hour][That day when evening came *(10:00 p.m.)*, When the sun was setting *(sunset)*, 'When Jesus heard that John had been put in prison he went out of the house *(home of Simon and Andrew the sons of Tanner)*. "Let us go over to the other side" *(Gennesaret shore region)*. That same day they got into the boat set off across the Sea of Galilee, returned to Galilee *(4th district of Galilee)* to a solitary place][Jesus crossed to the far shore of the Sea of Galilee. When he arrived at the other side in the region of the Gadarenes, they landed at Gennesaret and anchored there *(boats of Simon and Andrew, and James and John)*. When Jesus stepped ashore][**Jesus got out of the boat a man with an impure spirit**

came to meet him, he was met by a demon-possessed man from the town *(Judas the Gadarene)*]

{**Important note6:** There is a great revelation that will be revealed by Judas the Gadarene. To uncover the mystery, you must shift away from the Path of Jesus and follow the Path of Judas the Gadarene as he leads Jesus and his companions through the 4th district of Galilee, the district region called Gennesaret}

THE PATH OF JUDAS THE GADARENE

The first thing you must do is look closely at the bold portion in the following descriptions below,

Mark 5:15 - [**When they came to Jesus, they saw the man who had been possessed by the legion of demons**, sitting there, dressed and in his right mind; and **they were afraid]**

Luke 7:11- [Soon afterward, **Jesus went to a town called Nain**, and his disciples and a large crowd went along with him. As **he approached the town gate, a dead person was being carried out-the only son of his mother, and she was a widow.** And **a large crowd from the town was with her]**

Luke 9:37 - [The next day, **when they came down from the mountain, a large crowd met him. A man in the crowd called out, "Teacher, I beg you to look at my son, for he is my only child]**

Next, remove the following descriptions from the verses.

1- When they came to Jesus, they saw the man who had been possessed by the legion of demons
2- they were afraid
3- Jesus went to a town called Nain
4- he approached the town gate
5- a dead person was being carried out-the only son of his mother, and she was a widow
6- a large crowd from the town was with her
7- when they came down from the mountain
8- a large crowd met him
9- A man in the crowd called out, "Teacher, I beg you to look at my son, for he is my only child

Next, re-list the following descriptions removed from the verses.

- [he approached the town gate]

*(Note24: The following description above also reveals another vital clue. For example: The town gate corresponds to the great valley, known as the Valley of Sychar and represents the northeast entrance gate of Sychar (entering the town). This revelation corresponds to the bold portion of this description **'There were entrances to the side rooms from the open area, one on the north and another on the south;** and the base adjoining the open area was five cubits wide all around' – Ezekiel 41:11. The entrance gate represents the northeast entrance gate of Sychar as well as the southwest exit gate of Sychar and corresponds to the following two descriptions **'the gate of the town'** – 2 Samuel 18:4 (town called Sychar), and the **'town gate of the city'** – Luke 7:12 (city called Shechem). This area will be revealed in more detail moving forward))*

Here is the next clue: Judas the Gadarene leads Jesus and his companions to the northeast entrance gate of Sychar located at the following coastal region: [The coast of Tyre].

The next thing you must do is look closely at the bold portion in the following descriptions below,

Matthew 4:1 - [Then **Jesus was led by the Spirit into the desert** to be tempted **by the devil**]

Luke 4:1-2 - [Jesus, full of the Holy Spirit, returned from the Jordan and **was led by the Spirit in the desert**, where for forty days he was tempted **by the devil**]

Mark 1:12-13 - [At once **the Spirit sent him out into the desert**, and he was in the desert forty days, being tempted **by Satan**]

Next, remove the following descriptions from the verses. *See below,*

1- Jesus was led by the Spirit into the desert
2- by the devil
3- was led by the Spirit in the desert
4- by the devil
5- the Spirit sent him out into the desert
6- by Satan

*(Note26: The bold part of these descriptions 'Jesus was **led by the Spirit**' and 'the Spirit sent him out into the desert' is symbolic and reveals another major clue. For example: The 'Spirit' that leads Jesus corresponds to this description 'a man with an impure spirit came to meet him' - Mark 5:2. The following two descriptions '**by the devil**' and '**by Satan**' is also symbolic and corresponds to this description 'he was met by a demon-possessed man from the town' - Luke 8:27. Thus, the two revelations are also symbolic and corresponds to this description 'two demon possessed men coming from the tomb met him' – Matthew 8:28. Therefore, Jesus and his companions was led by one native, Judas the Gadarene)*

*(Note27: The '**desert**' is also symbolic and reveals a major clue. For example: The 'desert' corresponds to the northeast region of the valley of Sychar. This region land corresponds to the bold part of these descriptions: 'Jesus was led by the Spirit **into the desert**,' 'was led by the Spirit **in the desert**' and 'the Spirit **sent him out into the desert**.' The 'desert' represents the 'desert eastern hill region.' This revelation corresponds to the following two descriptions '**So Esau (that is, Edom) settled in the hill country of Seir**' – Genesis 36:8, and '**but Esau I have hated, and I have turned his hill country into a wasteland and left**'*

his inheritance to the desert jackals' – Malachi 1:3. Therefore, Judas the Gadarene leads Jesus and his companions from the northeast entrance gate of Sychar and journeyed towards the northeast region of the valley of Sychar (the desert Foothills) and led them to the top terrain section of the valley, known as the rugged terrain section (the desert hill region). This area will be revealed in more detail moving forward))

Here is the next clue: Judas the Gadarene leads Jesus and his companions from the northeast entrance gate *(the coast of Tyre)*, up the desert foothills, the northeast region of the valley of Sychar *(the top section of the valley)*, to the following coastal region: [The coast of Sidon].

{**Important note7:** The following two descriptions **'So Esau (that is, Edom) settled in the hill country of Seir'** – *Genesis 36:8*, and **'but Esau I have hated, and I have turned his hill country into a wasteland and left his inheritance to the desert jackals'** – *Malachi 1:3*, both corresponds to the coast of Sidon. The coast of Sidon corresponds to the top section of the valley of Sychar, the rugged terrain section of the valley, also called the desert hill region. Thus, Edom also is symbolic and corresponds to the coastal region of Sidon. Therefore, the hill country of Seir, corresponding to Edom *(the coast of Sidon)*, represents the west bank and east bank regions *(also called the wasteland regions)*. This area will be revealed in more detail moving forward}

Now, re-list the following description removed from the verses.

- [Jesus went to a town called Nain]

*(Note25: The 'town called Nain' is also symbolic and corresponds to the town called Sychar (northeast region of the Valley of Sychar, the west bank region). This revelation corresponds to the bold part of this description '**So he came to a town in Samaria called Sychar**, near the plot of ground Jacob had given to his son Joseph' – John 4:5 (the plot of ground is located at the southwest region of the valley of Sychar). This area will be revealed in more detail moving forward)*

Here is the next clue: Judas the Gadarene leads Jesus and his companions to the following region located at the top section of the valley of Sychar: [The west bank region, the town called Sychar]

The next thing you must do is look closely at the description below,

Acts 19:20 – [Then Herod went from Judea to Caesarea and stayed there. He had been quarreling with the people of Tyre and Sidon; they now joined together and sought an audience with him. After securing the support of Blastus, a trusted personal servant of the king, they asked for peace, because they depended on the king's country for their food supply.]

(Note30: This description is also written deceptively and reveals another trap! For example: Herod Lords over the land of the eastern hill country, the land of Samaria. He resides in the 4th district of Galilee, the region of Gennesaret and his palace is in the northeast region of the valley of Sychar, the desert hill region. Thus, this description 'Then Herod went from Judea to Caesarea and stayed there' is another deceptive trap! For example: Judea and Caesarea are symbolic and represent two regions that reside in two conflicting lands. The region of Judea resides in the western hill country, the land of Jerusalem. The region of Caesarea is symbolic and corresponds to Caesarea Philippi, which is also symbolic for representing the region of the Gadarenes, a region in the 4th district of Galilee, called Gennesaret (see page 97, of how Caesarea Philippi represents the region of the Gadarenes). Example2: As previously revealed, Herod does not reside in the region of the Gadarenes (revealed as Caesarea Philippi), he resides in the region of the Gerasenes. Therefore, the description 'Herod went from Judea (region land of the western hill country) to Caesarea (region of the Gadarenes) and stayed there' is a deceptive trap!)

Here is the next clue: King Herod resides at the northeast region of the valley of Sychar, in the coastal region of Sidon, in the following region: [The east bank region, the city called Shechem].

{**Important note8:** As revealed previously, the coast of Tyre represents the southwest region of the valley of Sychar, and the coast of Sidon represents the northeast region of the valley of Sychar. Therefore, the coast of Tyre and the coast of Sidon reside in the same district *(4th district of Galilee)*, in the same region *(region called Gennesaret)*, in the same land *(the land of Israel, the land of the Gentiles)*, and in the same country *(the eastern hill country, the land of Samaria)*. Therefore, this description *'they asked for peace, because they depended on the king's country for food'* is another deceptive trap!)

Next, re-list the following descriptions removed from the verses and look closely at the bold portion of the verses.

- [**a dead person was being carried out-the only son of his mother**, and she was a widow]
- [A man in the crowd called out, "Teacher, **I beg you to look at my son, for he is my only child**]

(Note28: The following two descriptions above also reveal another hidden clue. For example: The following description 'the only son of his mother' is symbolic and corresponds to the name of a man who represents the only son of his mother. Thus, the hidden clue is revealed by whom his mother corresponds to. Example2: The following description 'for he is my only child' is also symbolic and corresponds to the name of a man who represents the only son of his father. Thus, the hidden clue is revealed by whom his father corresponds to. This revelation will reveal the meaning behind this description 'Which way did he go?" And his sons showed him which road the man of God from Judah had taken' – 1st Kings 13:12.)

Here is the next clue: The dying boy *(only son of his father)* corresponds to the 'dead boy' *(only son of his mother)* and represents the following Man of God who came from Judah, who was beheaded: [John the Levite *(only son of his father Zechariah; and only son of his mother Elizabeth)*].

(Note29: The 'dead boy' and 'dying boy' are symbolic and corresponds to the beheading of John the son of Zechariah (known as John, the Levite). Thus, John the Levite was beheaded in the capital region city, known as the city, called Shechem (northeast region of the Valley of Sychar, the east bank region). This revelation corresponds to the following description 'Then all the elders of that city which is nearest to the slain man shall wash their hands over the heifer whose neck was broken in the valley' – Deuteronomy 21:6. The word 'heifer' is symbolic and corresponds to 'John, the Levite' (does not represent a Galilean, also called a Samaritan or Gentile). Thus, the word 'heifer' (though representing a female cow that has not borne a calf) is symbolic and corresponds to one as representing a descendant of Aaron (a Levite priest, from the land of the western hill country, the land of Jerusalem). Therefore, the word 'heifer' corresponds to this description 'Man of God who came from Judah.' This revelation also corresponds to the bold part of this description 'Our fathers worshiped on this mountain (the eastern hill country, the descendant land of Ephraim), but you Jews say that the place where one must worship is in Jerusalem (the western hill country land, the descendants of Judah).' – John 4:20. The 'Man of God who came from Judah' will be revealed more detail shortly. The 'dying boy' and 'dead boy,' carried out of the city corresponds to the

body of John the Levite (whose neck was broken in the valley). Thus, John was carried out of the capital region city called Shechem, the east bank region. The following description 'his neck was broken in the valley' corresponds to the northeast region of the valley of Sychar (the coast of Sidon))

(Note31: When John fled to the land of the eastern hill country, the land of Samaria, he did so to avoid arrest by the Temple guards sent by Annas and Caiaphas (Lords over the land of Jerusalem). Because John fled before he could be arrested, Caiaphas nursed a grudge against John and wanted to kill him (Thus, it was not Herodias who wanted John's head on a platter). Caiaphas consulted with Herod (upon Herod's return to the land of Jerusalem) on how to deal with the matter concerning John the Levite, who fled to the land of his jurisdiction, the eastern hill country. If you look closely at this description 'Does our law convict a man without first hearing from him to determine what he has done?'- John 7:51, you will discover the plot to deal with John the Levite was plotted in secret through their dealings with Herod, and not through the judicial process of convening a court, as would be the custom of the Jews revealed by the bold portion of this description – **'Those who had arrested Jesus took him to Caiaphas the high priest, where the teachers of the law and the elders had assembled. But Peter followed him at a distance, right up to the courtyard of the high priest**. He entered and sat down with the guards to see the outcome' – Matthew 26:57-58. The secret plot to have John murdered can also be revealed by merging the following two descriptions of Acts 12:11 and Luke 23:7, to understand the paradox between them. For example: **'rescued me from Herod's grasp** (who was also in Jerusalem at that time – Luke 23:7) **and from everything the Jewish people were anticipating'** (Annas and Caiaphas – Acts 12:11). Thus, king Herod would often frequent the land of Jerusalem to meet with Annas and Caiaphas, in Jerusalem the Holy City))

{**Important note9:** There is another hidden clue revealed in the verse of Luke 13:31, concerning the plot to have John murdered as well as John fleeing to the land of the eastern hill country. For example, if you look closely at this description **'At that time some Pharisees came to Jesus and said to him, "Leave this place and go somewhere else. Herod wants to kill you'** – Luke 13:31, you will discover a trap that reveals a hidden clue. For example: The word 'Pharisees' is symbolic and corresponds to the word, 'Levites.' Thus, representing a member in the school of the priesthood *(priestly division of Aaron)*, who represents a descendant of Aaron, who is baptized a Levite. The descendants of Aaron reside in the land of the western hill country, the land of Jerusalem. Herod, on the other hand, has no jurisdiction in the land of Jerusalem, because his jurisdiction is in the land of Samaria, the eastern hill country. Thus, he cannot execute, nor threaten to execute any native citizen living in the land of Jerusalem. Therefore, this description **'Leave this place and go somewhere else,'** does not correspond to King Herod's plot to kill Jesus *(a native of the* *eastern hill country, the land of the Gentiles)*, but corresponds to Caiaphas plot to have John the Levite killed *(a native of the western hill country, the land of the Jews)*. The region where John flees away from *(leave this place)* represents Jerusalem the Holy City. And this description *'and go somewhere else'* corresponds to the land of the eastern hill country, the land of Samaria *(John goes into exile to the land of the Gentiles)*}

*(Note32: The revelation attesting to the mindset of Caiaphas (wanting someone put to death) can also be revealed by this description '**Caiaphas was the one who had advised the Jewish leaders that it would be better if one man died for the people**' – John 18:12-14 (Though, it was not Jesus Caiaphas was referring too, it was John the Levite). The reason as to why Caiaphas wanted John to be put to death by Herod, instead of having him extradited back to the land of Jerusalem to be put to death can be summed up by the bold portion of this description 'Pilate said, "Take him yourselves and judge him by your own law." "**The Jews said to him, "It is not lawful for us to put anyone to death."**' – John 18:31. Therefore, it is not the custom of the Jews to execute any native citizen of the western hill country, who resides in the land of Jerusalem. And so, Herod, upon returning to the land of his jurisdiction, the eastern hill country, the land of Samaria, issued orders to have John, found, arrested, jailed, and killed! This revelation corresponds to this description 'So he immediately sent an executioner with orders to bring John's head. The man went, beheaded John in the prison' – Mark 6:27. This all happened in the 4th district of Galilee, the region called Gennesaret, at the northeast region of the valley of Sychar, the east bank region, the city called Shechem. The beheading of John served as proof to the delight of Caiaphas attesting to the death of John the Levite. Thus, Herod had John's head delivered to Caiaphas, the high priest! This revelation reveals the meaning behind this description 'and brought back his head on a platter' – Mark 6:28 (though, it was not the girl who was presented with John's head). On the contrary, it was Caiaphas, who received John's head on a platter from Herod as a gift))*

(Note33: John the Levite (came from the land of the Jews) represents the 'Man of God' who came from Judah (a descendant from the line of Judah). As revealed previously regarding the nation of Judah, the house and line of David as well as the descendants of Aaron, correspond to the descendants of Judah, who reside in the land of Jerusalem (the western hill country). However, the house and line of David as well as the descendants of Aaron (descendants of Judah) does not correspond to the land of Israel (descendant land of Ephraim). The descendant land of Ephraim represents the eastern hill country and correspond to the following four districts of Galilee: Nazareth, Capernaum, Bethsaida and Gennesaret, and represents the descendants of Esau, who resides in the land of Samaria (land of Israel). Therefore, Jesus does not

correspond to the term 'Man of God, who came from Judah' (land of the Jews) because he was born in the Kushite land of Egypt and raised in the custom of the Gentiles (called a Nazarene, a Galilean, a Samaritan, and a Gentile). John the Levite, on the other hand, corresponds to the description 'came from Judah' (land of the Jews) and represents the term 'Man of God.' Thus, the term **'Man of God'** is symbolic and corresponds to the word **'Levite,'** as representing a descendant of Aaron and one who belongs to the priestly division. Jesus the Nazarene does not belong to the priestly division of Aaron, nor is he a descendant of Aaron. Though, called a Nazarene, a Galilean, and a Samaritan, he will also be called a Gentile, not a prophet or a Man of God. This revelation fulfills the meaning behind this description **'They replied, "Are you from Galilee, too? Look into it, and you will find that a prophet does not come out of Galilee"'** - John 7:52. In other words, no Man of God (descendant of Aaron) comes from the land of the eastern hill country, the land of Samaria (land of the Gentiles). This revelation reveals the meaning behind this description **'Ephraim broke away from Judah'** – Isaiah 7:17)

Next, re-list the following descriptions removed from the verses.

- [When they came to Jesus, they saw the man who had been possessed by the legion of demons they were afraid]
- [a large crowd from the town was with her]
- [a large crowd met him]

(Note34: The 'large crowd from the town' reveals another major clue. For example: The large crowd from the town corresponds to the west bank and east bank regions that resides at the northeast region of the Valley of Sychar (the coast of Sidon))

Here is the next clue: The large crowd corresponds to the capital region city called Shechem *(east bank region)*, and the town called Sychar *(west bank region)* and represents the following citizens that reside at the northeast region of the valley of Sychar: [The region of the Gerasenes].

{**Important note10:** If you look closely at the description of the verses, *'**Then Jesus was led by the Spirit into the wilderness to be tempted by the devil. After fasting forty days and forty nights, he was hungry. The tempter came to him and said, "If you are the Son of God, tell these stones to become bread." Jesus answered, "It is written: 'Man shall not live on bread alone, but on every word that comes from the mouth of God'**'* – Matthew 4:1-4, you will discover it is another deceptive trap! For example: The Spirit does not represent an angel of sorts, nor does the tempter corresponds to the devil, nor Satan! Example2: The **'Spirit'** is symbolic and corresponds to the bold part of this description *'**a man with an impure spirit** came to meet him'* - Mark 5:2. The **'tempter'** is also symbolic and corresponds to the bold part of this description *'he was met by **a demon-possessed man** from the town'* - Luke 8:27. Example3: Both descriptions (Spirit = a man with an impure spirit) and (tempter = a demon-possessed man) are symbolic and correspond to the bold part of this description *'**two demon possessed men** coming from the tomb met him'* – Matthew 8:28. Therefore, Jesus was not led to the wilderness to be tempted, nor was he led by the spirit into the desert, but is led by Judas the Gadarene, to the northeast region of the valley of Sychar, the coast of Sidon, also known as the desert hill region}

125

The next thing you must do is merge the revelations together into the correct context.

- {Nation of Esau} = {Ten Horns} = [Ten kings = Ten tribes: *(Ephraim, Manasseh, Naphtali, Dan, Asher, Issachar, Zebulon, Simeon, Reuben, and Gad)* = Nation of Ephraim = *who are yet to receive a kingdom of their own* = Kingdom of Samaria = Conquered by the Assyrian Empire = Exodus by the Kushite Empire *(Wadi of Egypt)*] = [2nd Exodus] = {Descendants of Esau} = {Eastern hill country} = {Land of Samaria} = {Land of Israel} = {Land of the Gentiles} = [1st District of Galilee = District region of Nazareth *(Joseph, Mary and Jesus exiled)*] = [2nd District of Galilee = District region of Capernaum *(Land of Zebulun and land of Naphtali, the way to the sea, along the Jordan)*] = [3rd District of Galilee = District region of Bethsaida *(Philip, Nathanael, Simon, Andrew, James, John, Zacchaeus and Levi)* = Bethsaida Shore region of Galilee] = [4th District of Galilee = District region of Gennesaret *(coasts of Tyre and Sidon)* = Gennesaret Shore region of Galilee *(Sea of Tiberias)*] = [Region of the Gadarenes: *(Caesarea Philippi)* = *(Judas the Gadarene)*] = **[Region of the Gerasenes: Town called Sychar *(west bank region)* and Capital region city called Shechem *(east bank region)*]**

- {Nation of Jacob} = {Beast} = [single tribe: *(Benjamin)* = Nation of Judah = *remained in the city* = Conquered by Babylonian Empire = Exodus by the Persian Empire] = [2nd Exodus] = [Kingdom of Jerusalem] = {Descendants of Jacob} = {Western hill country} = {Land of Jerusalem} = {Land of the Jews} = [Hill country of Judea: *(Zechariah, Elizabeth and John son of Zechariah)*] = [Region of Judea: *(Joseph and Mary)*] = [Capital region of Jerusalem = Jerusalem the Holy City: *(John becomes a Levite priest before the Temple courts)*] = [Region of Bethany *(less than two miles from Jerusalem the Holy City)*]

The next thing you must do is look closely at the bold portion in the following descriptions below,

Mark 9:14-16 - [When they came to **the other disciples, they saw a large crowd around them** and the teachers of the law **arguing with them**. As soon as all the people saw Jesus, they were overwhelmed with wonder and ran to greet him. "What are you **arguing with them** about?" he asked]

Mark 9:33 - [They came to Capernaum. When he was in the house, he asked them, "What were you **arguing** about **on the road**?]

Luke 9:46 - [An **argument started among the disciples** as to which of them would be the greatest]

John 3:25 - [**An argument developed between some of John's disciples** and a certain Jew over the matter of ceremonial washing]

Next, re-list the following descriptions removed from the verses.

- [arguing with them]
- [arguing on the road]
- [argument started among the disciples]
- [An argument developed between some of John's disciples]

*(Note35: The following descriptions also reveal another major clue. For example: The road they argued upon corresponds to one of the three terrain sections of the valley of Sychar. The three sections of the valley correspond to the bold part of this description 'Every valley shall be raised up, every mountain and hill made low; **the rough ground shall become level, the rugged places a plain**' - Isaiah 40:4. Thus, the 'rugged terrain' corresponds to the top section of the valley of Sychar, the 'rough terrain' corresponds to the middle section of the valley of Sychar and the 'leveled terrain' corresponds to the level section of the valley of Sychar. Therefore, the top section (rugged terrain) corresponds to the northeast region of the valley of Sychar (the coast of Sidon), and the level section (level terrain) corresponds to the southwest region of the valley of Sychar (the coast of Tyre). These three sections of the valley are also referred to as the desert Foothills. These three sections of the valley of Sychar will be revealed in more detail throughout the 3rd Chronicles series. The top section of the valley of Sychar (rough terrain) as representing the northeast region of the valley of Sychar, and the level section of the valley of Sychar (leveled terrain) as*

representing the southwest region of the valley of Sychar, corresponds to the following description *'Then people go to their eternal home (southwest region of the valley of Sychar) and mourners go about the streets'* (northeast region of the valley of Sychar) – Ecclesiastes 12:5. For example: This part of the description 'mourners go about the streets' corresponds to the west bank region of the Gerasene (town called Sychar) and the east bank region of the Gerasene (city called Shechem). The west bank and east bank regions also correspond to the following description **'down the middle of the great street of the city'** (east and west bank regions) – Revelation 22:2. This area (middle of the great street), is revealed by Mount Gerizim and Mount Ebal. Thus, the great street of the city is divided by two mountains (mountain of the north and mountain of the south). This revelation will also be revealed in more detail throughout the 3rd Chronicle series. Example2: This part of the description 'Then people go to their eternal home' is symbolic and corresponds to the southwest region of the Valley of Sychar (as representing the burial place, also known as the plot of ground Jacob, gave to his son Joseph). This revelation also corresponds to the following description **'the cave in the field of Machpelah** (the southwest region of the valley of Sychar)**, near Mamre in Canaan** (the northeast region of the valley of Sychar)**, which Abraham bought along with the field as a burial place from Ephron the Hittite** (the level terrain section of the valley of Sychar)- Genesis 49:30. This revelation will also be revealed in more detail throughout the 3rd Chronicle series. The northeast and southwest regions of the valley also correspond to this description **"Enter through the narrow gate** (northeast entrance gate of Sychar)**. For wide is the gate (**as representing the northeast region of the valley of Sychar, the top section of the valley, the coast of Sidon**) and broad is the road** (east and west bank regions of the Gerasenes) **that leads to destruction, and many enter through it** (Mount Gerizim and Mount Ebal)**. But small is the gate** (the southwest exit gate of Sychar, the level terrain section of the valley, the coast of Tyre) **and narrow the road** (the southwest region of the valley of Sychar, also known as the Western Foothills) **that leads to life, and only a few find it'** – Matthew 7:13-14. These revelations will also be revealed in more detail in the 3rd Chronicle series.)

(Note36: The argument that erupts on the road between the large crowd (the east bank region of the Gerasene) and among the following companions of John the Levite (Zacchaeus and Levi, the sons of Alphaeus), erupts over the arrest and death of their companion with the citizens of the east bank region of the Gerasene (the city called Shechem) because John's deceased body was carried out of the city, with his head no longer attached to his body))

Next, re-list the following description removed from the verses.

- [the other disciples, they saw a large crowd around them]

*(Note37: The 'other disciples' is symbolic and correspond to the following companions of Jesus: **Philip, Nathanael, Simon and Andrew the sons of Tanner and James and John the sons of Zebedee.** Thus, two boats set sail during the 10th hour and anchored in the Shore region of Gennesaret at the 11th hour)*

The next thing you must do is look closely at the bold portion in the following descriptions below,

Matthew 8:34 - [Then **the whole town** went out to meet Jesus. And when they saw him, they **pleaded with him to leave their region**]

Luke 8:37 - [Then all **the people of the region of the Gerasenes asked Jesus to leave them, because they were overcome with fear**]

Mark 5:17 - [**Then the people began to plead with Jesus to leave their region**]

The next thing you must do is remove the following descriptions from the verses. *See below,*

1- the whole town pleaded with him to leave their region
2- the people of the region of the Gerasenes asked Jesus to leave them because they were overcome with fear
3- Then the people began to plead with Jesus to leave their region

*(Note38: The following descriptions above also reveals a hidden clue. For example: This description 'leave their region' corresponds to the west bank region of the Gerasenes, known as the town, called Sychar. This revelation corresponds to the bold descriptions of the verse '**When they came to Jesus, they saw the man who had been possessed by the legion of demons**, sitting there, dressed and in his right mind; **and they were afraid**' – Mark 5:15. Thus, the man possessed by the legion of demons corresponds to the following description 'demon-possessed man from the town.' This revelation corresponds to Judas the Gadarene (the demon-possessed man from the town) as representing the man in the description '**they saw the man who had been possessed by the legion of demons.**')*

129

(Note39: An argument also erupts on the road between the large crowd (east bank region of the Gerasenes) and Jesus the Nazarene over the beheading of his relative John the son of Zechariah because John's body was carried out of the city, with his head no longer attached to his body. This revelation reveals the meaning behind this description **'the people of the region of the Gerasenes asked Jesus to leave them because they were overcome with fear.'** *The west bank region of the Gerasenes became overcome with fear because an argument erupts, not only with John's companions, but also with Jesus, with the citizens of the east bank region of the Gerasenes as John's deceased body was carried out of the city. Thus, it was Judas the Gadarene who led Jesus and his companions to their region land (the west bank region), and they pleaded with them to leave!))*

The next thing you must do is re-list the entire descriptions removed from the verses and place the bold descriptions in the correct number order according to the context of the story.

[57] **When they came to Jesus, they saw the man who had been possessed by the legion of demons**

[62] **they were afraid**

[52] **Jesus went to a town called Nain**

[53] **he approached the town gate**

[54] **a dead person was being carried out-**the only son of his mother, and she was a widow

[55] **a large crowd from the town** was with her

when they came down from the mountain

a large crowd met him

A man in the crowd called out, "Teacher, I beg you to look at my son, for he is my only child

[61] **the other disciples, they saw a large crowd around them**

arguing with them

arguing [59] **on the road**

argument started among the disciples

[58] **An argument developed** [60] **between some of John's disciples**

the [64] **whole town pleaded** with him to leave their region

the people [56] **of the region of the Gerasenes** asked Jesus to leave them [63] **Then the** people began to plead [65] **with Jesus to leave their region**

Next, remove the bold descriptions in numbered order and construct them into the correct context as seen below,

[52] Jesus went to a town called Nain [53] he approached the town gate [54] a dead person was being carried out [55] a large crowd from the town [56] of the region of the Gerasenes [57] When they came to Jesus, they saw the man who had been possessed by the legion of demons [58] An argument developed [59] on the road [60] between some of John's disciples [61] the other disciples, they saw a large crowd around them [62] they were afraid [63] Then the [64] whole town pleaded [65] with Jesus to leave their region

To reveal the tenth piece to the sacred document of Immanuel you must merge the revelations into the correct context as seen below,

[Leaving Nazareth *(1ˢᵗ district of Galilee)*, he went in Capernaum *(2ⁿᵈ district of Galilee)* Land of Zebulun and land of Naphtali, the way to the sea *(Sea of Galilee)*, along the Jordan *(Jordan River)*] [The next day Jesus decided to leave for the town of Bethsaida *(3ʳᵈ district of Galilee)*] [Now Philip was from Bethsaida, Philip found Nathanael and told him -Jesus of Nazareth, the son of Joseph."][As Jesus walked beside the Sea of Galilee, *(accompanied by Philip and Nathanael)* he saw at the water's edge *(Bethsaida shore region)* two boats, left there by the fishermen *(companions of Philip and Nathanael)*. He saw two brothers - Simon and his brother Andrew, who were washing their nets and asked him to put out a little from shore *(sail beyond the Bethsaida shore region limit)*. He got into one of the boats, the one belonging to Simon *(accompanied by Andrew, Philip and Nathanael)*. Put out into deep water and let down the nets for a catch *(sail to the Gennesaret shore region)*][When he *(Simon)* had gone a little farther, he saw two other brothers, James's son of Zebedee and his brother John *(fishing companions)* in a boat, preparing their nets. Going on from there, *(crossing the Bethsaida border into the Gennesaret region)* his companions *(Simon, Andrew, Philip and Nathanael)* were astonished at the catch of fish they had taken, and so were James and John, the sons of Zebedee *(native companions from the Bethsaida region)* Simon's partners.' So they signaled their partners in the other boat *(James and John -sons of Zebedee)* to come and help them, and they came *(from Bethsaida shore region)* and filled both boats so full that they began to sink *(Gennesaret shore region)*][When the two disciples *(Zacchaeus and Levi the sons of Alphaeus)* heard him say this, they followed Jesus *(returned to Bethsaida)*. Turning around, Jesus saw them following. When the men came to Jesus, they said, "John *(your relative)* sent us to you "where are you staying?" "Come," he replied, "and you will see". So they went and saw where he was staying *(home of Simon and Andrew, the sons of Tanner)*. It was about the tenth hour][That day when evening came *(10:00 p.m.)*, When the sun was setting *(sunset)*, 'When Jesus heard that John had been put in prison he went out of the house *(home of Simon and Andrew the sons of Tanner)*. "Let us go over to the other side" *(Gennesaret shore region)*. That same day they got into the boat set off across the Sea of Galilee, returned to Galilee *(4ᵗʰ district of Galilee)* to a solitary place][Jesus crossed to the far shore of the Sea of Galilee. When he arrived at the other side in the region of the Gadarenes, they landed at Gennesaret and anchored there *(boats of Simon and Andrew, and James and John)*. When Jesus stepped ashore][Jesus got out of the boat a man with an impure spirit came to meet him, he was met by a demon-possessed man from the town *(Judas the Gadarene)*][**Jesus**

132

went to a town called Nain *(town called Sychar)* he approached the town gate *(northeast entrance gate of Sychar)* a dead person was being carried out *(John the Levite)* a large crowd from the town *(west bank and east bank regions)* of the region of the Gerasenes. When they came to Jesus, they saw the man who had been possessed by the legion of demons *(Judas the Gadarene)*. An argument developed on the road *(coast of Sidon)* between some of John's disciples *(Zacchaeus and Levi)* the other disciples, *(Philip, Nathanael, Simon, Andrew, James and John)* they saw a large crowd around them they were afraid. Then the whole town pleaded with Jesus to leave their region *(west bank region of the Gerasenes)*]

The next thing you must do is look closely at the bold portion in the following descriptions below,

, Matthew 17:1 - [After six days Jesus took with him Peter, James and John the brother of James, and **led them up a high mountain by themselves**]

Mark 9:2 - [After six days Jesus took Peter, James and John with him and **led them up a high mountain, where they were all alone**]

Luke 9:28 - [About eight days after Jesus said this, he took Peter, John and James with him and **went up onto a mountain** to pray]

Next, remove the following descriptions from the verses.

1- led them up a high mountain by themselves
2- led them up a high mountain, where they were all alone
3- went up onto a mountain

(Note40: The following descriptions above reveal another major clue. For example: This high mountain represents the highest mountain that resides in the 4th district of Galilee, the region of Gennesaret. This high mountain is known as Mount Ebal (as representing the mountain of Esau, the cursed mountain). Mount Ebal towers 3,084 feet (940 meters) above sea level and towers 194 feet (59 meters) above Mount Gerizim, the mountain of the north (as also representing the mountain of Jacob, the blessed mountain). Mount Ebal also towers approximately 6.5 square miles, equivalent to 18 square kilometers and resides on the east bank region of the Gerasenes, also known as the city, called Shechem))

Here is the final clue: The high mountain corresponds to Mount Ebal and represents the following high mountain that resides in the 4th district of Galilee at the northeast region of the valley of Sychar: [The mountain of the south].

{**Important note11:** This High Mountain represents the highest mountain in the land of Samaria *(the eastern hill country)* and corresponds to the bold part of this description regarding the Samaritan woman, **'Our fathers worshiped on this mountain'** – John 4:20. Therefore, this High Mountain *(as representing Mount Ebal, the mountain of the south)* represents the Mountain of God}

(Note41: The bold portion of this description **'the devil took him** *to a very high mountain' - Matthew 4:8, is written deceptively and reveals a hidden clue. For example: The* **'devil'** *in this description is symbolic and corresponds to the bold portion of this description* **'he was met by a demon-possessed man** *from the town.' And the bold portion of this description 'Jesus was* **led by the Spirit** *into the desert' is also symbolic and corresponds to the bold portion of this description* **'an impure spirit came from the tombs to meet him.'** *Therefore, the words 'devil' and 'Spirit' are both symbolic and corresponds to the bold portion of this description* **'two demon-possessed men** *coming from the tombs met him.' Thus, they correspond to Judas the Gadarene (man from the town). This revelation corresponds to the following description* **'the man who had been possessed by the legion of demons.'** *Judas the Gadarene leads Jesus along the High Mountain of the south to the southwest region of the Valley of Sychar (direction leading towards the burial place))*

(Note42: The southwest region of the valley of Sychar and the northeast region of the valley of Sychar (The Foothills) corresponds to this description **'He led me back and forth among them, and I saw a great many bones on the floor of the valley, bones that were very dry'** *– Ezekiel 37:2)*

The next thing you must do is look closely at the bold portion in the following descriptions below,

1- Mark 5:2 - [When Jesus got out of the boat, a man with an impure spirit **came from the tombs** to meet him]
2- Matthew 8:28 - [When he arrived at the other side in the region of the Gadarenes, two demon-possessed men **coming from the tombs** met him]

(Note43: The word **'tomb'** *in both descriptions is symbolic and reveals another major clue. For example: The tomb corresponds to the mountain of the south (as corresponding to the plot of ground Jacob gave to his son Joseph). This area represents the level terrain section of the valley and corresponds to this description* **'the base adjoining the open area was five cubits wide all around'** *– Ezekiel 41:11.' This revelation will be revealed in more detail shortly)*

The next thing you must do is re-list the entire descriptions removed from the verses and place the bold descriptions in the correct number order according to the context of the story.

[67] **led them up a high mountain by themselves**

led them up a high mountain, [68] **where they were all alone**

went up onto a mountain

Next, remove the descriptions in the numbered order and construct them into the correct context as seen below,

[67] led them up a high mountain by themselves [68] where they were all alone

To reveal the eleventh piece to the sacred document of Immanuel you must merge the revelations into the correct context as seen below,

[Leaving Nazareth *(1st district of Galilee)*, he went in Capernaum *(2nd district of Galilee)* Land of Zebulun and land of Naphtali, the way to the sea *(Sea of Galilee)*, along the Jordan *(Jordan River)*] [The next day Jesus decided to leave for the town of Bethsaida *(3rd district of Galilee)*] [Now Philip was from Bethsaida, Philip found Nathanael and told him -Jesus of Nazareth, the son of Joseph."][As Jesus walked beside the Sea of Galilee, *(accompanied by Philip and Nathanael)* he saw at the water's edge *(Bethsaida shore region)* two boats, left there by the fishermen *(companions of Philip and Nathanael)*. He saw two brothers - Simon and his brother Andrew, who were washing their nets and asked him to put out a little from shore *(sail beyond the Bethsaida shore region limit)*. He got into one of the boats, the one belonging to Simon *(accompanied by Andrew, Philip and Nathanael)*. Put out into deep water and let down the nets for a catch *(sail to the Gennesaret shore region)*][When he *(Simon)* had gone a little farther, he saw two other brothers, James's son of Zebedee and his brother John *(fishing companions)* in a boat, preparing their nets. Going on from there, *(crossing the Bethsaida border into the Gennesaret region)* his companions *(Simon, Andrew, Philip and Nathanael)* were astonished at the catch of fish they had taken, and so were James and John, the sons of Zebedee *(native companions from the Bethsaida region)* Simon's partners.' So they signaled their partners in the other boat *(James and John -sons of Zebedee)* to come and help them, and they came *(from Bethsaida shore region)* and filled both boats so full that they began to sink *(Gennesaret shore region)*][When the two disciples *(Zacchaeus and Levi the sons of Alphaeus)*

136

heard him say this, they followed Jesus *(returned to Bethsaida)*. Turning around, Jesus saw them following. When the men came to Jesus, they said, "John *(your relative)* sent us to you "where are you staying?" "Come," he replied, "and you will see". So they went and saw where he was staying *(home of Simon and Andrew, the sons of Tanner)*. It was about the tenth hour][That day when evening came *(10:00 p.m.)*, When the sun was setting *(sunset)*, 'When Jesus heard that John had been put in prison he went out of the house *(home of Simon and Andrew the sons of Tanner)*. "Let us go over to the other side" *(Gennesaret shore region)*. That same day they got into the boat set off across the Sea of Galilee, returned to Galilee *(4th district of Galilee)* to a solitary place][Jesus crossed to the far shore of the Sea of Galilee. When he arrived at the other side in the region of the Gadarenes, they landed at Gennesaret and anchored there *(boats of Simon and Andrew, and James and John)*. When Jesus stepped ashore][Jesus got out of the boat a man with an impure spirit came to meet him, he was met by a demon-possessed man from the town *(Judas the Gadarene)*][Jesus went to a town called Nain *(town called Sychar)* he approached the town gate *(northeast entrance gate of Sychar)* a dead person was being carried out *(John the Levite)* a large crowd from the town *(west bank and east bank regions)* of the region of the Gerasene. When they came to Jesus, they saw the man who had been possessed by the legion of demons *(Judas the Gadarene)*. An argument developed on the road *(coast of Sidon)* between some of John's disciples *(Zacchaeus and Levi)* the other disciples, *(Philip, Nathanael, Simon, Andrew, James and John)* they saw a large crowd around them they were afraid. Then the whole town pleaded with Jesus to leave their region *(west bank region of the Gerasenes)*][***(Judas the Gadarene)* led them up a high mountain, *(mountain of the south)* by themselves where they were all alone *(southwest region of the Valley of Sychar)*]**

The next thing you must do is look closely at the bold portion in the following descriptions below,

Matthew 17:4 - [Peter said to Jesus, "Lord, it is good for us to be here. If you wish, **I will put up three shelters**-one for you, one for Moses and one for Elijah]

Luke 9:33 - [As the men were leaving Jesus, Peter said to him, "Master, it is good for us to be here. **Let us put up three shelters**-one for you, one for Moses and one for Elijah]

Mark 9:5 - [Peter said to Jesus, "Rabbi, it is good for us to be here. **Let us put up three shelters**-one for you, one for Moses and one for Elijah]

Next, remove the following descriptions from the verses.

1- I will put up three shelters
2- Let us put up three shelters

*(Note44: The following descriptions above also reveal another hidden clue. For example: The word 'shelter' is symbolic and corresponds to the word 'tomb' (Thus, there are not three shelters; but one tomb). This revelation will be revealed in more detail in the 3rd Chronicle series of the Elijah Doctrine. The tomb also corresponds to the bold part of this description 'What are you doing here and who gave you permission **to cut out a grave for yourself here, hewing your grave on the height and chiseling your resting place in the rock?**'– Isaiah 22:16. Thus, the rock corresponds to the base (adjoining the open area). This revelation will be revealed in more detail moving forward as well as the 3rd Chronicle series. To reveal the clue, you must look closely at the following descriptions of Matthew 14:12 and Mark 6:29)*

Look closely at the bold portion of the following two descriptions below,

Matthew 14:12 - [**John's disciples came and took his body and buried it**. Then they went and told Jesus]

Mark 6:29 – [On hearing of this, **John's disciples came and took his body and laid it in a tomb**]

Here is the final revelation: The word 'shelter' corresponds to a 'cut-out tomb with a stone laid across the entrance' and represents the burial place of the Man of God who came from the land of Jerusalem *(descendants of Judah)*: [The Tomb of John the Levite].

(Note45: The 'tomb' of John the Levite (Man of God who came from Judah) corresponds to the bold part of this description 'Jesus came to the tomb. ***It was a cave with a stone laid across the entrance'*** *– John 11:38. To understand this better, merge part of the description of Isaiah 22:16 and 2ⁿᵈ Kings 23:17 together to see the paradox between them. For example:* ***'The king asked, "What is that tombstone I see?"*** *(hewing your grave on the height)* ***The people of the city said, "It marks the tomb of the man of God who came from Judah'*** *(Chiseling your resting place in the rock) – 2ⁿᵈ* ***Kings 23:17.*** *This revelation corresponds to the following description* ***'the base adjoining the open area was five cubits wide all around.'*** *The base adjoining the open area is symbolic and represents a large Rock that blocks the entrance of the valley. This revelation reveals the meaning behind this description* ***'It will block the way of travelers'*** *- Ezekiel 39:11.)*

{**Important note12:** As revealed previously, the mountain of the south, as representing the High Mountain *(also known as Mount Ebal)*, represents the mountain of God and corresponds to this description ***'Our fathers worshiped on this mountain'*** – John 4:20. The base adjoining the open area *(five cubits wide all around)* as representing a large Rock that blocks the entrance of the valley is also symbolic and represents the mountain of the Lord *(also known as the sacred mountain)* and corresponds to this description ***'We ourselves heard this voice that came from heaven when we were with him on the sacred mountain'*** – 2ⁿᵈ Peter 1:18}

(Note46: Jesus and his companions take possession of John's body from the citizens of the east bank region of the Gerasenes, the city called Shechem (mountain of the south), and journeyed down the Western Foothills (as representing the three terrain sections of the valley: the rugged terrain, the rough terrain, and the level terrain), revealed as the southwest region of the valley of Sychar and gave John the Levite a proper burial at the large Rock that blocks the entrance of the valley (the coast of Tyre). Thus, the base (five cubits wide all around) corresponding to the large Rock that blocks the entrance of the valley, resembles the appearance of a tombstone shaped mountain. This area will be revealed in more detail moving forward))

{**Important note13:** If you look closely at the description of the verses, *'Again, the devil took him to a very high mountain and showed him all the kingdoms of the world and their splendor. "All this I will give you," he said, "if you will bow down and worship me." Jesus said to him, "Away from me, Satan! For it is written: 'Worship the Lord your God and serve him only'* – Matthew 4:8-10, you will discover it too, is a deceptive trap! For example: The high mountain represents the highest mountain in the land of the eastern hill country. Mount Ebal (mountain of the south) towers over any mountain found in either of the two lands, the land of Jerusalem and the land of Samaria. Therefore, it was not the devil that took Jesus up the High Mountain. It was Judas the Gadarene who led Jesus to the High Mountain, mountain of the south *(from the northeast region of the valley of Sychar)* and to the Large Rock that blocks the entrance of the valley *(to the southwest region of the valley of Sychar)*, also known as the base adjoining the open area *(five cubits wide all around)*, the level terrain section of the valley}

The next thing you must do is look closely at the bold portion in the following descriptions below,

Mark 9:9-10 - [**As they were coming down the mountain, Jesus gave them orders not to tell anyone what they had seen** until the Son of Man had risen from the dead. They kept the matter to themselves, discussing what "rising from the dead" meant]

Luke 9:36 - [When the voice had spoken, they found that Jesus was alone. **The disciples kept this to themselves, and told no one** at that time what they had seen]

Luke 9:37 - [The next day, **when they came down from the mountain,** a large crowd met him]

Matthew 17:9 - [**As they were coming down the mountain, Jesus instructed them, "Don't tell anyone what you have seen,** until the Son of Man has been raised from the dead]

Luke 6:17-18 - [**He went down with them and stood on a level place**. A large crowed of his disciples was there and a great number of people from all over Judea, from Jerusalem, and from **the coast of Tyre and Sidon,** who had come to hear him and to be healed of their diseases]

Next, remove the following descriptions from the verses.

1- As they were coming down the mountain, Jesus gave them orders not to tell anyone what they had seen
2- The disciples kept this to themselves, and told no one
3- when they came down from the mountain
4- As they were coming down the mountain, Jesus instructed them, "Don't tell anyone what you have seen
5- He went down with them and stood on a level place
6- the coast of Tyre and Sidon

Next, re-list the following description removed from the verses.

[the coast of Tyre and Sidon]

*(Note47: The burial place of John the Levite (cut-out tomb with a stone laid across the entrance) corresponds to the bold portion of this description 'demon-possessed man **coming from the tomb**.' Thus, the burial place corresponds to the coast that borders the coastal region of the Gerasenes (the coast of Sidon). The border across from the coast of Sidon represents the southwest region of the Valley of Sychar and represents the coast of Tyre. This revelation corresponds to the bold part of this description 'After burying him, he said to his sons, "When I die, **bury me in the grave where the man of God is buried**; lay my bones beside his bones' – 1ˢᵗ Kings 13:31. The grave is symbolic and corresponds to this description **'the plot of ground Jacob had given to his son Joseph** – John 4:1-7. This area represents the level terrain section of the valley and corresponds to this description **'there was a garden, and in the garden a new tomb'** – John 19:41. John the Levite was buried in the coastal region of Tyre at the level terrain section of the valley, in the garden that faces the large Rock that blocks the entrance of the valley (tombstone shaped mountain). This area will be revealed in more detail moving forward))*

Here is the next clue: The '**base adjoining the open area**' as corresponding to a '**large Rock**' that blocks the entrance of the valley, located at the '**level terrain section of the valley, the coast of Tyre,**' represents the following place: [The Foot of the Mountain *(tombstone shaped mountain)*]

The next thing you must do is re-list the entire descriptions removed from the verses and place the bold descriptions in the correct number order according to the context of the story.

I will put up three shelters

[69] **Let us put up** three [70] **shelters**

[71] **John's disciples came and took his body and buried it**

As they were coming down the mountain, Jesus gave them orders not to tell anyone what they had seen

[73] **The disciples kept this to themselves,** and told no one

when they came down from the mountain

[72] **As they were coming down the mountain,** Jesus instructed them, "Don't tell anyone what you have seen

[74] **He went down with them and stood on a level place**

[75] **the coast of Tyre** and Sidon

Next, remove the descriptions in the numbered order and construct them into the correct context as seen below,

[69] Let us put up [70] shelters [71] John's disciples came and took his body and buried it [72] As they were coming down the mountain [73] The disciples kept this to themselves [74] He went down with them and stood on a level place

To reveal the twelfth piece to the sacred document of Immanuel you must merge the revelations into the correct context as seen below,

[Leaving Nazareth *(1st district of Galilee)*, he went in Capernaum *(2nd district of Galilee)* Land of Zebulun and land of Naphtali, the way to the sea *(Sea of Galilee)*, along the Jordan *(Jordan River)*] [The next day Jesus decided to leave for the town of Bethsaida *(3rd district of Galilee)*] [Now Philip was from Bethsaida, Philip found Nathanael and told him -Jesus of Nazareth, the son of Joseph."][As Jesus walked beside the Sea of Galilee, *(accompanied by Philip and Nathanael)* he saw at the water's edge *(Bethsaida shore region)* two boats, left there by the fishermen *(companions of Philip and Nathanael)*. He saw two brothers - Simon and his brother Andrew, who were washing their nets and asked him to put out a little from shore *(sail beyond the Bethsaida shore region limit)*. He got into one of the boats, the one belonging to Simon *(accompanied by Andrew, Philip and Nathanael)*. Put out into deep water and let down the nets for a catch *(sail to the Gennesaret shore region)*][When he *(Simon)* had gone a little farther, he saw two other brothers, James's son of Zebedee and his brother John *(fishing companions)* in a boat, preparing their nets. Going on from there, *(crossing the Bethsaida border into the Gennesaret region)* his companions *(Simon, Andrew, Philip and Nathanael)* were astonished at the catch of fish they had taken, and so were James and John, the sons of Zebedee *(native companions from the Bethsaida region)* Simon's partners.' So they signaled their partners in the other boat *(James and John -sons of Zebedee)* to come and help them, and they came *(from Bethsaida shore region)* and filled both boats so full that they began to sink *(Gennesaret shore region)*][When the two disciples *(Zacchaeus and Levi the sons of Alphaeus)* heard him say this, they followed Jesus *(returned to Bethsaida)*. Turning around, Jesus saw them following. When the men came to Jesus, they said, "John *(your relative)* sent us to you "where are you staying?" "Come," he replied, "and you will see". So they went and saw where he was staying *(home of Simon and Andrew, the sons of Tanner)*. It was about the tenth hour][That day when evening came *(10:00 p.m.)*, When the sun was setting *(sunset)*, 'When Jesus heard that John had been put in prison he went out of the house *(home of Simon and Andrew the sons of Tanner)*. "Let us go over to the other side" *(Gennesaret shore region)*. That same day they got into the boat set off across the Sea of Galilee, returned to Galilee *(4th district of Galilee)* to a solitary place][Jesus crossed to the far shore of the Sea of Galilee. When he arrived at the other side in the region of the Gadarenes, they landed at Gennesaret and anchored there *(boats of Simon and Andrew, and James and John)*. When Jesus stepped ashore][Jesus got out of the boat a man with an impure spirit came to meet him, he was met by a demon-possessed man from the town *(Judas the Gadarene)*][Jesus

144

went to a town called Nain *(town called Sychar)* he approached the town gate *(northeast entrance gate of Sychar)* a dead person was being carried out *(John the Levite)* a large crowd from the town *(west bank and east bank regions)* of the region of the Gerasenes. When they came to Jesus, they saw the man who had been possessed by the legion of demons *(Judas the Gadarene)*. An argument developed on the road *(coast of Sidon)* between some of John's disciples *(Zacchaeus and Levi)* the other disciples, *(Philip, Nathanael, Simon, Andrew, James and John)* they saw a large crowd around them they were afraid. Then the whole town pleaded with Jesus to leave their region *(west bank region of the Gerasenes)*][*(Judas the Gadarene)* led them up a high mountain, *(mountain of the south)* by themselves where they were all alone *(southwest region of the Valley of Sychar)*][**Let us put up shelters** *(what is that tombstone I see)***. John's disciples came and took his body and buried it** *(marks the tomb of the man of God who came from Judah)***. As they were coming down the mountain** *(Foot of the Mountain)***. The disciples** *(companions)* **kept this to themselves. He went down with them and stood on a level place** *(level terrain section of the valley)*]

*(Note48: The following description '***stood on a level place***' is symbolic and corresponds to the coast of Tyre. This revelation corresponds to the bold portion of this description 'every mountain and hill made low; **the rough ground shall become level**, the rugged places a plain' – Isaiah 40:4. Thus, the 'level place' corresponds to the level terrain section of the valley)*

{**Important note14:** The burial of John the Levite *(buried absent his head)*, reveals the meaning behind this description '***The people of the city said, "It marks the tomb of the man of God who came from Judah'*** – 2nd Kings 23:17 *(as representing the tomb of the headless man, a descendant of Aaron)*. Thus, the base adjoining the open area, as representing a large Rock that blocks the entrance of the valley, and revealed as the Foot of the Mountain, represents the tombstone shaped mountain. This revelation reveals the meaning behind this description '***The king asked, "What is that tombstone I see?"*** – 2nd Kings 23:17. Therefore, the people of the city, corresponds to the northeast region of the valley of Sychar, the east bank region of the Gerasenes, the city called Shechem, and the king, corresponds to king Herod *(presides as lord over the land of the eastern hill country, the land of Samaria)*}

145

The final thing you must do is merge the revelations together regarding the coasts of Tyre and Sidon into the correct context.

- {Nation of Esau} = {Ten Horns} = [Ten kings = Ten tribes: *(Ephraim, Manasseh, Naphtali, Dan, Asher, Issachar, Zebulon, Simeon, Reuben, and Gad)* = Nation of Ephraim = *who are yet to receive a kingdom of their own* = Kingdom of Samaria = Conquered by the Assyrian Empire = Exodus by the Kushite Empire *(Wadi of Egypt)*] = [2nd Exodus] = {Descendants of Esau} = {Eastern hill country} = {Land of Samaria} = {Land of Israel} = {Land of the Gentiles} = [1st District of Galilee = District region of Nazareth *(Joseph, Mary and Jesus exiled)*] = [2nd District of Galilee = District region of Capernaum *(Land of Zebulun and land of Naphtali, the way to the sea, along the Jordan)*] = [3rd District of Galilee = District region of Bethsaida *(Philip, Nathanael, Simon, Andrew, James, John, Zacchaeus and Levi)* = Bethsaida Shore region of Galilee] = [4th District of Galilee = District region of Gennesaret *(region of Tyre and Sidon)* = Gennesaret Shore region of Galilee *(Sea of Tiberias)*] = [Region of the Gadarenes: *(Caesarea Philippi)* = *(Judas the Gadarene)* = **Southwest region of the valley of Sychar = Coast of Tyre *(Foot of the Mountain)***] = [**Northeast region of the valley of Sychar = Coast of Sidon** = Region of the Gerasenes: Town called Sychar *(west bank region)* and Capital region city called Shechem *(east bank region)*}

- {Nation of Jacob} = {Beast} = [single tribe: *(Benjamin)* = Nation of Judah = *remained in the city* = Conquered by Babylonian Empire = Exodus by the Persian Empire] = [2nd Exodus] = [Kingdom of Jerusalem] = {Descendants of Jacob} = {Western hill country} = {Land of Jerusalem} = {Land of the Jews} = [Hill country of Judea: *(Zechariah, Elizabeth and John son of Zechariah)*] = [Region of Judea: *(Joseph and Mary)*] = [Capital region of Jerusalem = Jerusalem the Holy City: *(John becomes a Levite priest before the Temple courts)*] = [Region of Bethany *(less than two miles from Jerusalem the Holy City)*]

Congratulations! You have successfully revealed the 3rd and 4th woes hidden behind the 3rd and 4th miraculous signs:

….. **Jesus was not led to the desert and Tempted by the Devil; but was led up the desert Foothills, the northeast region of the Valley of Sychar, to the top section of the valley, the rugged terrain level, the coast of Sidon, known as the desert hill region, the region of the Gerasenes, by Judas the Gadarene, to recover the body of his slain relative, John the son of Zechariah, from the citizens of the east bank region, the city called Shechem** …..

….. **Jesus was not Transfigured on the High Mountain; but was led to the High Mountain, the mountain of the south, down the Western Foothills, revealed as the southwest region of the Valley of Sychar, by Judas the Gadarene, to the base adjoining the open area, the level terrain section of the valley, the coast of Tyre, to bury John the Levite** *(The Man of God who came from Judah)* **on the large Rock that blocks the entrance of the valley, revealed as the Foot of the Mountain, the tombstone shaped mountain**…...

CHAPTER FOUR- 2ND PHASE OF THE CRYPTEX PUZZLE- THE PATH OF THE SIGN

The fifth and sixth tests in this Chapter is to unveil the mystery revealed behind the [5th and 6th woes] by revealing the revelation concealed behind the 5th and 6th miraculous signs: [**Lazarus raised from the tomb**] and [**The Crucifixion of Jesus**]!

(Note: In this chapter, you must continue to follow the Path of Judas the Gadarene as he continues to lead Jesus and his companions through the southwest region of the Valley of Sychar)

The next thing you must do is look closely at the bold portion in the following descriptions below,

Luke 10:38-39 - [**As Jesus and his disciples were on their way, he came to a village where a woman named Martha opened her home to him. She had a sister called Mary**, who sat at the Lord's feet listening to what he said]

Luke 16:20 - [**At his gate was laid a beggar named Lazarus**, covered with sores]

John 12:17 - [Now the crowd that was with him when he called **Lazarus from the tomb** and raised him from the dead continued to spread the word]

John 11:1-2 - [Now a man named **Lazarus** was sick. He **was from Bethany, the village of Mary and her sister Martha.** This Mary, whose brother Lazarus now lay sick, was the same one who poured perfume on the Lord and wiped his feet with her hair]

John 11:17 - [On his arrival, Jesus found that **Lazarus had already been in the tomb** for four days]

John 11:43 - [**Jesus**, once more deeply moved, **came to the tomb. It was a cave with a stone laid across the entrance**]

John 21:1-2 - [Six days before the Passover, **Jesus arrived at Bethany, where Lazarus lived**, whom Jesus had raised from the dead. Here **a dinner was given in Jesus' honor. Martha served, while Lazarus was among those reclining at the table with him**]

Next, remove the following descriptions from the verses.

1- As Jesus and his disciples were on their way, he came to a village where a woman named Martha opened her home to him She had a sister called Mary
2- At his gate was laid a beggar named Lazarus
3- Lazarus from the tomb
4- Lazarus was from Bethany, the village of Mary and her sister Martha
5- Lazarus had already been in the tomb
6- Martha and Mary brother
7- Jesus came to the tomb. It was a cave with a stone laid across the entrance
8- Jesus arrived at Bethany, where Lazarus lived
9- Here a dinner was given in Jesus' honor. Martha served
10- This Mary was the same one who poured perfume on the Lord and wiped his feet with her hair

Next, re-list the following descriptions removed from the verses.

4- [Lazarus was from Bethany, the village of Mary and her sister Martha]
5- [Martha and Mary brother]
6- [Jesus arrived at Bethany, where Lazarus lived]

(Note2: The following descriptions above reveal three major clues. For example: The region of Bethany, as previously revealed, represents a region in the western hill country, the land of Jerusalem (land of the Jews). Thus, the region of Bethany corresponds to the following description 'Bethany was less than two miles from Jerusalem' – John 11:18 (traveling west outside of Jerusalem the Holy City))

(Note3: The village of Mary and her sister Martha does not correspond to the land of the Jews (the western hill country); but correspond to the land of the Gentiles (the eastern hill country). Thus, the 'village' corresponds to one of the following two region lands that make-up the 4th district of Galilee, the Region of the Gerasenes (northeast region of the valley of Sychar) or the Region of the Gadarenes (southwest region of the valley of Sychar). This revelation will reveal the meaning behind this description **'Jesus left that place and went to the vicinity of Tyre. He entered a house'** *– Mark 7:24))*

150

(Note4: The 'village of Mary and Martha' corresponds to the coast of Tyre (southwest region of the Valley of Sychar) and represents the village, called Ephraim (located in the vicinity of Tyre). This area corresponds to the bold portion of this description 'Instead __he withdrew to a region__ near the wilderness, __to a village called Ephraim, where he stayed with his disciples__' – John 11:54. The 'village called Ephraim' is symbolic and corresponds to the region of the Gadarenes (as representing the open area). Thus, this description 'near the wilderness' is symbolic and corresponds to the northeast region of the valley of Sychar (also known as the wasteland or the desert hill region). The northeast region of the valley (the desert wilderness) also corresponds to the bold portion of this description 'but Esau I have hated, __and I have turned his hill country into a wasteland and left his inheritance to the desert jackals__' – Malachi 1:3. The southwest and northeast region of the valley also corresponds to the bold portion of this description 'Now a Levite who lived in a remote area in the hill country of Ephraim (southwest region of the valley of Sychar, as representing the open area) took a concubine from Bethlehem in Judah (west bank region, the northeast region of the valley of Sychar) – Judges 19:1)

Here is the next clue: The village of Mary and Martha corresponds to the Village called Ephraim and represents the following remote region located at the southwest region of the valley of Sychar, the vicinity of Tyre: [The open field *(adjacent to the base adjoining the open area, the region of the Gadarenes)*].

{**Important note:** The "open area" corresponds to the "open field" and represents the vicinity of Tyre. Therefore, the word **"vicinity"** corresponds to the word **"adjoining."** Thus, it is the base *(large Rock that blocks the entrance of the valley)* adjoining the open area *(open field)*, revealed as the Foot of the Mountain that represents the coast of Tyre. The open area also corresponds to the following two descriptions: *'After that, he is to release the live bird in the open fields (vicinity of Tyre)'* – Leviticus 14:7, and *'Then he is to release the live bird in the open fields (the region of the Gadarenes) outside the town (town called Sychar)'* – Leviticus 14:53. This region will be revealed in more detail throughout the 3rd Chronicle series}

(Note5: This revelation corresponds to this description __'he withdrew to a region near the wilderness__ (southwest region of the valley of Sychar, the coast of Tyre), __to a village called Ephraim__ (the open field, near the base adjoining the open area, the vicinity of Tyre)__, where he stayed with his disciples'__ (the region of the Gadarenes). This revelation reveals the meaning behind this description __'Jesus left that place__ (the level terrain section of the valley, the coast of Tyre) __and went to the vicinity of Tyre__ (the region of the Gadarenes, the village called Ephraim). __He entered a house'__ (home of Mary and Martha) – Mark 7:24. This revelation will be revealed in more detail shortly.)

{**Important note2:** If you recall from the previous revelations revealed in the 1st Chronicle, The Elijah Doctrine *(Revelation of the Sign)* regarding the nation of Ephraim, you will discover another hidden clue revealed in the description of John 11:54. For example: The following revelations: [**ten horns = ten crowns = ten kings = ten tribes = Nation of Ephraim *(land of Israel)* = Kingdom of Samaria *(descendants of Esau)***], revealed in the 1st Chronicle of the Elijah Doctrine, also correspond to the following ten natives traveling through the land of Samaria who have settled in a remote village within the 4th district of Galilee: **Philip, Nathanael, Simon, Andrew, James, John, Zacchaeus, Levi, Jesus and Judas the Gadarene** *(ten natives gathered together in the village called Ephraim)*. To illustrate this, bring back the revelations revealed in the 1st Chronicle, the Elijah Doctrine *(Revelation of the Sign)* and merge the new revelations in the correct place}

Look carefully at the illustration below regarding the previous revelations revealed by the 1st Chronicle of the Elijah Doctrine and merged the new revelations regarding the four districts of Galilee, and the ten natives from the land of Samaria, the land of the Gentiles, in the correct place as seen below,

{4TH prominent horn} = [7TH head = 7TH hill = 7TH king] = [4TH beast (ten horns) = 4TH kingdom = City of David] = [Divided Kingdom]:

- {Ten Horns} = {Nation of Esau} = [Ten tribes = *I will take the kingdom from his son's hands and give you ten tribes* = Tribes of: Ephraim, Manasseh, Naphtali, Dan, Asher, Issachar, Zebulon, Simeon, Reuben, and Gad] = [Ten crowns = Ten kings = Nation of Ephraim = King Jeroboam = *who are yet to receive a kingdom of their own* = Kingdom of Samaria] = [Conquered by the Assyrian Empire] = [Exodus by the Kushite Empire *(Wadi of Egypt)*] = {Descendants of Esau} = {Eastern hill country} = {Land of Samaria} = {Land of Israel} = {Land of the Gentiles} = [1st District of Galilee = Region of Nazareth] = [2nd District of Galilee = Region of Capernaum] = [3rd District of Galilee = Region of Bethsaida] = [**4th District of Galilee = Region of Gennesaret**] = {**Ten traveling natives: *Philip, Nathanael, Simon, Andrew, James, John, Zacchaeus, Levi, Jesus and Judas the Gadarene* = Southwest region of the valley of Sychar = Village called Ephraim = Region of the Gadarenes**]

Next, remove the following descriptions from the verses.

7- [Lazarus from the tomb]

8- [Lazarus had already been in the tomb]

9- [Jesus came to the tomb. It was a cave with a stone laid across the entrance]

*(Note6: The name Lazarus is symbolic and corresponds to the bold portion of this description 'a man with an impure spirit **came from the tombs to meet him**' – Mark 5:2. For example: The 'tomb of Lazarus' is symbolic and corresponds to the bold part of this description '**At his gate** was laid a beggar named Lazarus.' The '**gate**' is symbolic and corresponds to the entrance gate of Sychar (called the town gate). The '**town gate**' is also symbolic and represents the northeast entrance gate of Sychar (when entering the town) as well as the southwest exit gate of Sychar (when exiting the town). Thus, the word 'tomb' is located near the 'town gate.' This revelation corresponds to the bold portion of this description '**There were entrances to the side rooms from the open area, one on the north and another on the south**' – Ezekiel 41:11. Therefore, it is the tomb that corresponds to this description '**and the base adjoining the open area was five cubits wide all around**' – Ezekiel 41:11. This revelation also corresponds to the bold portion of this description '**"What is that tombstone I see?" The people of the city** (northeast region of the valley of Sychar, the east bank region of the Gerasenes, the city called Shechem) **said, "It marks the tomb of the man of God who came from Judah'** (the southwest region of the valley of Sychar) – 2nd Kings 23:17))*

*(Note7: The word 'tomb' is symbolic and corresponds to the word 'base' (five cubits wide all around) as representing a large Rock that blocks the entrance of the valley and represents the Foot of the Mountain, revealed as the tombstone shaped mountain. This area also corresponds to the following description '**the plot of ground Jacob gave to his son Joseph,**' also known as the burial place or garden of the tomb, located at the level terrain section of the valley)*

*(Note8: The **tomb** (large rock rolled over the mouth of the cave) corresponding to the **base** (five cubits wide all around) as representing a **large Rock** (tombstone shaped mountain), also corresponds to the bold portion of this description 'And besides all this, **between us and you a great chasm has been set in place, so that those who want to go from here** (southwest region of the valley) **to you cannot, nor can anyone cross over from there** (northeast region of the valley) **to us '** – Luke 16:26. Therefore, the 'base adjoining the open area (five cubits wide all around) corresponds to the 'great chasm.' This revelation also corresponds to the bold portion of this description '**This heap is a witness, and this pillar is a witness** (large Rock that blocks the entrance of the valley), **that I will not go past this heap to your side to harm***

153

you (northeast region of the Valley of Sychar) **and that you will not go past this heap and pillar to my side to harm me** (southwest region of the Valley of Sychar) - *Genesis 31:52. This revelation reveals the meaning behind this description* **'It will block the way of travelers** - *Ezekiel 39:11. This revelation will be revealed in more detail very shortly as well as throughout the 3rd Chronicle series))*

The next thing you must do is look closely at the bold portion in the following descriptions below,

> John 12:2-3 - [**Here a dinner was given in Jesus' honor. Martha served, while Lazarus was among those reclining at the table with him.** Then Mary took about a pint of pure nard, an expensive perfume; she poured it on Jesus' feet and wiped his feet with her hair. And the house was filled with the fragrance of the perfume]

> Mark 14:3 - [While he was in Bethany, **reclining at the table in the home of a man known as Simon the Leper**, a woman came with a alabaster jar expensive perfume]

Next, remove the following descriptions from the verses.

> 11- [Here a dinner was given in Jesus' honor. Martha served, while Lazarus was among those reclining at the table with him]

> 12- [reclining at the table in the home of a man known as Simon the Leper]

(Note9: The following descriptions also reveal a vital clue. For example: The home of Simon the Leper is symbolic and corresponds to the home of Lazarus. Example2: The following two names Lazarus (from the village of Bethany) and Simon the Leper (also from the village of Bethany) are written deceptively and correspond to the bold part of this description 'two demon-possessed men coming from the tomb' – Matthew 8:28. Thus, 'Lazarus' corresponds to this description 'demon-possessed' as well as correspond to the bold part of this description 'he was met by a demon-possessed man from the town' – Luke 8:27. And 'Simon the Leper' corresponds to the description 'impure spirit' as well as correspond to the bold part of this description 'a man with an impure spirit came from the tombs to meet him' – Mark 5:2. The two names 'Lazarus' and 'Simon the Leper' are symbolic and corresponds to the name of one native living near the tomb in the vicinity of Tyre)

To illustrate this, look closely at the illustration below regarding the previous revelations and merge the new revelations in the correct places as seen below,

- {1ˢᵗ demon-possessed man} = [a man with an impure spirit = Satan entered Judas] = [**Iscariot = Simon the Leper**]

- {2ⁿᵈ demon-possessed man} = [many demons had gone into him] = [**Legion = Lazarus**]

*(Note10: The following two names: **'Judas called Iscariot'** ("Very truly I tell you, one of you is going to betray me – John 13:21) and **'Simon the Leper'** (And they scolded her. – Mark 14:4) both corresponds to this description 'a man with an impure spirit – Mark 5:2.')*

*(Note11: The following two names: **'Legion'** (they saw the man who had been possessed by the legion of demons, sitting there, dressed and in his right mind – Mark 5:15) and **'Lazarus'** (At his gate was laid a beggar named Lazarus, covered with sores – Luke 16:20) both corresponds to this description 'a demon-possessed man – Luke 8:27'))*

Here is the next clue: The following two descriptions [Legion = Lazarus = a demon-possessed man] and [Iscariot = Simon the Leper = a man with an impure spirit] corresponds to the description *'two demon-possessed men came from the tomb'* and represents the following description 'he was met by a demon-possessed man from the town' as representing the following true native living in the vicinity of Tyre *(near the northeast entrance gate of Sychar)* within the village called Ephraim: [Judas the Gadarene].

The next thing you must do is merge the revelations together regarding the 'village called Ephraim' and the 'vicinity of Tyre' into the correct context.

- {Nation of Esau} = {Ten Horns} = [Ten kings = Ten tribes: *(Ephraim, Manasseh, Naphtali, Dan, Asher, Issachar, Zebulon, Simeon, Reuben, and Gad)* **=** Nation of Ephraim = *who are yet to receive a kingdom of their own* = Kingdom of Samaria = Conquered by the Assyrian Empire = Exodus by the Kushite Empire *(Wadi of Egypt)*] = [2nd Exodus] = {Descendants of Esau} **=** {Eastern hill country} = {Land of Samaria} = {Land of Israel} = {Land of the Gentiles} = [1st District of Galilee = District region of Nazareth *(Joseph, Mary and Jesus exiled)*] = [2nd District of Galilee = District region of Capernaum *(Land of Zebulun and land of Naphtali, the way to the sea, along the Jordan)*] = [3rd District of Galilee = District region of Bethsaida *(Philip, Nathanael, Simon, Andrew, James, John, Zacchaeus and Levi)* = Bethsaida Shore region of Galilee] = [4th District of Galilee = District region of Gennesaret *(region of Tyre and Sidon)* = Gennesaret Shore region of Galilee *(Sea of Tiberias)*] = [Region of the Gadarenes: *(Caesarea Philippi)* = *(Judas the Gadarene)* = Southwest region of the valley of Sychar = Coast of Tyre *(Foot of the Mountain)* = **Vicinity of Tyre = Village called Ephraim** *(open field, open area)*] = [Northeast region of the valley of Sychar = Coast of Sidon = Region of the Gerasenes: Town called Sychar *(west bank region)* and Capital region city called Shechem *(east bank region)*]

- {Nation of Jacob} = {Beast} = [single tribe: *(Benjamin)* **=** Nation of Judah = *remained in the city* = Conquered by Babylonian Empire = Exodus by the Persian Empire] = [2nd Exodus] = [Kingdom of Jerusalem] = {Descendants of Jacob} **=** {Western hill country} = {Land of Jerusalem} = {Land of the Jews} = [Hill country of Judea: *(Zechariah, Elizabeth and John son of Zechariah)*] = [Region of Judea: *(Joseph and Mary)*] = [Capital region of Jerusalem = Jerusalem the Holy City: *(John becomes a Levite priest before the Temple courts)*] = [Region of Bethany *(less than two miles from Jerusalem the Holy City)*]

Next, re-list the final description removed from the verses.

- [This Mary was the same one who poured perfume on the Lord and wiped his feet with her hair]
- [Here a dinner was given in Jesus' honor. Martha served]

*(Note12: The two descriptions above reveal two hidden clues. For example: There is a paradox revealed between these two descriptions and the verse of Ezekiel 9:4. Example2: The dinner is symbolic and corresponds to the death of John the Levite (thus, Martha **grieves** with John's companions over the death of their friend). And the wiping of Jesus feet (with her hair) is symbolic and correspond to the death of John the son of Zechariah (thus, Mary **laments** with Jesus over the death of his relative). The two revelations (Martha grieves) and (Mary laments) correspond to this description 'those who grieve and lament over all the detestable things that are done in it' – Ezekiel 9:4. Thus, Martha (grieves) and Mary (laments) corresponds to the detest killing of John the Levite (the Man of God who came from Judah). This revelation reveals the meaning behind this description '**he withdrew to a region near the wilderness, to a village called Ephraim, where he stayed with his disciples**' – John 11:54 (as representing the open field, also called the open area). This revelation also reveals the meaning behind this description '**Then all the elders of that city** (east bank region of the Gerasenes, the city called Shechem) **which is nearest to the slain man** (southwest region of the valley of Sychar, the coast of Tyre) **shall wash their hands over the heifer** (Man of God who came from Judah) **whose neck was broken in the valley** (northeast region of the valley of Sychar, the coast of Sidon)' – Deuteronomy 21:6)*

Here is the 1st clue: The **'prepared dinner'** corresponds to the word **'grieve'** and symbolizes the following meaning: [Martha prepares a dinner for Judas's companions in honor of John the Levite, the Man of God who came from Judah].

Here is the 2nd clue: The **'wiping of Jesus feet with hair'** corresponds to the word **'lament'** and symbolizes the following meaning: [Mary mourns with Jesus over the death of his relative, John the son of Zechariah].

The next thing you must do is re-list the entire descriptions removed from the verses and place the bold descriptions in the correct number order according to the context of the story.

[75] **As Jesus and his disciples were on their way,** [79] **he came to a village** where [81] **a woman named Martha opened her home to him. She had a sister called Mary**

[78] **At his gate** was laid a beggar named Lazarus

Lazarus [76] **from the tomb**

Lazarus was from Bethany, [80] **the village of Mary and her sister Martha**

Lazarus had already been in the tomb

[83] **Martha and Mary brother**

Jesus came to the tomb. It was [77] **a cave with a stone laid across the entrance**

Jesus arrived at Bethany, where Lazarus lived

[82] **Here a dinner was given in honor.** Martha [84] **served**

This Mary was the same one who poured perfume on the Lord and wiped his [90] **feet with her hair**

[85] **While he was** in Bethany, [86] **reclining at the table** in the home of a man known as Simon the Leper

[87] **Then Mary** took about a pint of pure nard, an expensive perfume; she poured it [89] **on Jesus**

This Mary was the same one who [88] **poured perfume** on the Lord [91] **and wiped his feet with her hair**

Next, remove the descriptions in the numbered order and construct them into the correct context as seen below,

[75] As Jesus and his disciples were on their way, [76] from the tomb [77] a cave with a stone laid across the entrance [78] At his gate [79] he came to a village [80] the village of Mary and her sister Martha [81] a woman named Martha opened her home to him. [822] Here a dinner was given in honor [83] Martha and Mary brother [84] served [85] While he was [86] reclining at the table [87] Then Mary [88] poured perfume [89] on Jesus [90] feet with her hair [91] and wiped his feet with her hair

To reveal the thirteenth piece to the sacred document of Immanuel you must merge the revelations into the correct context as seen below,

[Leaving Nazareth *(1st district of Galilee)*, he went in Capernaum *(2nd district of Galilee)* Land of Zebulun and land of Naphtali, the way to the sea *(Sea of Galilee)*, along the Jordan *(Jordan River)*] [The next day Jesus decided to leave for the town of Bethsaida *(3rd district of Galilee)*] [Now Philip was from Bethsaida, Philip found Nathanael and told him -Jesus of Nazareth, the son of Joseph."][As Jesus walked beside the Sea of Galilee, *(accompanied by Philip and Nathanael)* he saw at the water's edge *(Bethsaida shore region)* two boats, left there by the fishermen *(companions of Philip and Nathanael)*. He saw two brothers - Simon and his brother Andrew, who were washing their nets and asked him to put out a little from shore *(sail beyond the Bethsaida shore region limit)*. He got into one of the boats, the one belonging to Simon *(accompanied by Andrew, Philip and Nathanael)*. Put out into deep water and let down the nets for a catch *(sail to the Gennesaret shore region)*][When he *(Simon)* had gone a little farther, he saw two other brothers, James's son of Zebedee and his brother John *(fishing companions)* in a boat, preparing their nets. Going on from there, *(crossing the Bethsaida border into the Gennesaret region)* his companions *(Simon, Andrew, Philip and Nathanael)* were astonished at the catch of fish they had taken, and so were James and John, the sons of Zebedee *(native companions from the Bethsaida region)* Simon's partners.' So they signaled their partners in the other boat *(James and John -sons of Zebedee)* to come and help them, and they came *(from Bethsaida shore region)* and filled both boats so full that they began to sink *(Gennesaret shore region)*][When the two disciples *(Zacchaeus and Levi the sons of Alphaeus)* heard him say this, they followed Jesus *(returned to Bethsaida)*. Turning around, Jesus saw them following. When the men came to Jesus, they said, "John *(your relative)* sent us to you "where are you staying?" "Come," he replied, "and you will see". So they went and saw where he was staying *(home of Simon and Andrew, the sons of Tanner)*. It was about the tenth hour][That day when evening came *(10:00 p.m.)*, When the sun was setting *(sunset)*, 'When Jesus heard that John had been put in prison he went out of the house *(home of Simon and Andrew the sons of Tanner)*. "Let us go over to the other side" *(Gennesaret shore region)*. That same day they got into the boat set off across the Sea of Galilee, returned to Galilee *(4th district of Galilee)* to a solitary place][Jesus crossed to the far shore of the Sea of Galilee. When he arrived at the other side in the region of the Gadarenes, they landed at Gennesaret and anchored there *(boats of Simon and Andrew, and James and John)*. When Jesus stepped ashore][Jesus got out of the boat a man with an impure spirit came to meet him, he was met by a demon-possessed man from the town *(Judas the Gadarene)*][Jesus

160

went to a town called Nain *(town called Sychar)* he approached the town gate *(northeast entrance gate of Sychar)* a dead person was being carried out *(John the Levite)* a large crowd from the town *(west bank and east bank regions)* of the region of the Gerasene. When they came to Jesus, they saw the man who had been possessed by the legion of demons *(Judas the Gadarene)*. An argument developed on the road *(coast of Sidon)* between some of John's disciples *(Zacchaeus and Levi)* the other disciples, *(Philip, Nathanael, Simon, Andrew, James and John)* they saw a large crowd around them they were afraid. Then the whole town pleaded with Jesus to leave their region *(west bank region of the Gerasenes)*][*(Judas the Gadarene)* led them up a high mountain, *(mountain of the south)* by themselves where they were all alone *(southwest region of the Valley of Sychar)*][Let us put up shelters *(what is that tombstone I see)*. John's disciples came and took his body and buried it *(marks the tomb of the man of God who came from Judah)*. As they were coming down the mountain *(Foot of the Mountain)*. The disciples *(companions)* kept this to themselves. He went down with them and stood on a level place *(level terrain section of the valley)*][**As Jesus and his disciples were on their way, from the tomb a cave with a stone laid across the entrance *(base adjoining the open area)*. At his gate *(southwest exit gate of Sychar, the coast of Tyre)* he came to a village the village of Mary and her sister Martha *(village called Ephraim)* a woman named Martha opened her home to him. Here a dinner was given in honor *(Man of God who came from Judah)*. Martha and Mary brother served *(grieves over the death of John the Levite)*. While he was reclining at the table. Then Mary poured perfume on Jesus feet with her hair and wiped his feet with her hair *(laments with Jesus over the death of his slain relative John son of Zechariah)*]**

The next thing you must do is look closely at the bold portion in the following descriptions below,

John 19:25 - [Near the cross of Jesus stood his mother, his mother's sister, **Mary the wife of Clopas, and Mary Magdalene]**

Matthew 27:56 - [Among them were **Mary Magdalene, Mary the mother of James and Joses, and the mother of Zebedee's son]**

Matthew 27:61 - [**Mary Magdalene and the other Mary** were sitting there opposite the tomb]

Matthew 28:1 - [After the Sabbath, at dawn on the first day of the week, **Mary Magdalene and the other Mary** went to look at the tomb]

Mark 15:47 - [**Mary Magdalene and Mary the mother of Jesus** saw where he was laid]

Mark 15:40 - [Some women were watching from a distance. Among them were **Mary Magdalene, Mary the mother of James the younger and of Joses, and Salome]**

Luke 24:10 - [It was **Mary Magdalene, Joanna, Mary the mother of James**, and the others with them who told this to the apostles]

Next, remove the following descriptions from the verses.

1- Mary the wife of Clopas, and Mary Magdalene
2- Mary Magdalene, Mary the mother of James and Joses, and the mother of Zebedee's son
3- Mary Magdalene and the other Mary
4- Mary Magdalene, Mary the mother of James the younger and of Joses, and Salome
5- Mary Magdalene, Joanna, Mary the mother of James

(Note13: The following descriptions above reveal two very important clues. To uncover the clue, you must reveal two hidden clues within each of the descriptions above. Their revelations will reveal the truth to what never took place regarding the death of Jesus!)

Next, re-list the following description removed from the verses.

- [Mary the wife of Clopas, and Mary Magdalene]

(Note14: The following description above reveals two hidden clues. For example: Mary (the wife of Clopas) is symbolic and corresponds to the word 'elder.' Example2: Mary Magdalene is also symbolic and corresponds to the word 'younger.')

Here is the 1st clue: **Mary** the wife of Clopas corresponds to the word 'elder' and represents the following elder sister: [Martha]

Here is the 2nd clue: **Mary Magdalene** corresponds to the word 'younger' and represents the following younger sister: [Mary]

Next, re-list the following description removed from the verses.

- [Mary Magdalene, Mary the mother of James and Joses, and the mother of Zebedee's son]

*(Note15: The following description above reveals two hidden clues. For example: Mary (mother of Zebedee's son) is symbolic and corresponds to the word 'elder' (does not represent the name of Zebedee's wife). Example2: Mary Magdalene is also symbolic and corresponds to the word 'younger.' The following name however, **'Joses'** is written deceptively and does not represent one of the sons of Zebedee (James and John the sons of Zebedee))*

Here is the 1st clue: **Mary** the mother of James and Joses, and the mother of Zebedee's son corresponds to the word 'elder' and represents the following elder sister: [Martha]

Here is the 2nd clue: **Mary Magdalene** corresponds to the word 'younger' and represents the following younger sister: [Mary]

163

Next, re-list the following description removed from the verses.

- [Mary Magdalene and the other Mary]

(Note16: The following description above reveals two hidden clues. For example: Mary (the other Mary) is symbolic and corresponds to the word 'elder.' Example2: Mary Magdalene is also symbolic and corresponds to the word 'younger.')

Here is the 1ˢᵗ clue: The **other Mary** corresponds to the word 'elder' and represents the following elder sister: [Martha]

Here is the 2ⁿᵈ clue: **Mary Magdalene** corresponds to the word 'younger' and represents the following younger sister: [Mary]

Next, re-list the following description removed from the verses.

- [Mary Magdalene, Mary the mother of James the younger and of Joses, and Salome]

*(Note17: The following description above reveals two hidden clues. For example: Mary (the mother of James the younger and of Joses, and Salome) is symbolic and corresponds to the word 'elder.' Example2: Mary Magdalene is also symbolic and corresponds to the word 'younger.' Thus, the following names however, **'Joses and Salome'** is written deceptively and does not represent the sons of Zebedee (James the younger and John the elder, sons of Zebedee))*

Here is the 1ˢᵗ clue: **Mary** the mother of James the younger and of Joses, and Salome corresponds to the word 'elder' and represents the following elder sister: [Martha]

Here is the 2ⁿᵈ clue: **Mary Magdalene** corresponds to the word 'younger' and represents the following younger sister: [Mary]

Next, re-list the following description removed from the verses.

- [Mary Magdalene, Joanna, Mary the mother of James]

(Note18: The following description above reveals two hidden clues. For example: Mary (the mother of James) is symbolic and corresponds to the word 'elder.' Example2: Mary Magdalene is also symbolic and corresponds to the word 'younger.' Thus, the following name 'Joanna' represents the mother of James and John the sons of Zebedee. Therefore, she represents the wife of Zebedee))

Here is the 1st clue: **Mary** the mother of James corresponds to the word 'elder' and represents the following elder sister: [Martha]

Here is the 2nd clue: **Mary Magdalene** corresponds to the word 'younger' and represents the following younger sister: [Mary]

Here is the final clue: **Martha the elder sister** and **Mary the younger sister** represents the following sisters of Judas the Gadarene from the region of the Gadarenes: [Mary and Martha, the Gadarenes].

*(Note19: The following two names, 'Lazarus' and 'Simon the Leper' do not represent the brothers of Mary and her sister Martha. These two names are symbolic and only correspond to the bold part of this description '**two demon-possessed men**.' Therefore, Judas the Gadarene represents the true brother of Mary and Martha, the Gadarenes, (he represents the middle sibling))*

The next thing you must do is merge the revelations together into the correct context.

- {Nation of Esau} = {Ten Horns} = [Ten kings = Ten tribes: *(Ephraim, Manasseh, Naphtali, Dan, Asher, Issachar, Zebulon, Simeon, Reuben, and Gad)* = Nation of Ephraim = *who are yet to receive a kingdom of their own* = Kingdom of Samaria = Conquered by the Assyrian Empire = Exodus by the Kushite Empire *(Wadi of Egypt)*] = [2nd Exodus] = {Descendants of Esau} = {Eastern hill country} = {Land of Samaria} = {Land of Israel} = {Land of the Gentiles} = [1st District of Galilee = District region of Nazareth *(Joseph, Mary and Jesus exiled)*] = [2nd District of Galilee = District region of Capernaum *(Land of Zebulun and land of Naphtali, the way to the sea, along the Jordan)*] = [3rd District of Galilee = District region of Bethsaida *(Philip, Nathanael, Simon, Andrew, James, John, Zacchaeus and Levi)* = Bethsaida Shore region of Galilee] = [4th District of Galilee = District region of Gennesaret *(coast of Tyre and Sidon)* = Gennesaret Shore region of Galilee *(Sea of Tiberias)*] = [Region of the Gadarenes: *(Caesarea Philippi)* = *(Judas, **Mary and Martha the Gadarenes**)* = Southwest region of the valley of Sychar = Coast of Tyre *(Foot of the Mountain)* = Vicinity of Tyre = Village called Ephraim *(open field, open area)*] = [Northeast region of the valley of Sychar = Coast of Sidon = Region of the Gerasenes: Town called Sychar *(west bank region)* and Capital region city called Shechem *(east bank region)*]

- {Nation of Jacob} = {Beast} = [single tribe: *(Benjamin)* = Nation of Judah = *remained in the city* = Conquered by Babylonian Empire = Exodus by the Persian Empire] = [2nd Exodus] = [Kingdom of Jerusalem] = {Descendants of Jacob} = {Western hill country} = {Land of Jerusalem} = {Land of the Jews} = [Hill country of Judea: *(Zechariah, Elizabeth and John son of Zechariah)*] = [Region of Judea: *(Joseph and Mary)*] = [Capital region of Jerusalem = Jerusalem the Holy City: *(John becomes a Levite priest before the Temple courts)*] = [Region of Bethany *(less than two miles from Jerusalem the Holy City)*]

{**Important note3:** If you look closely at the description of the verses, '***When Jesus saw his mother there, and the disciple whom he loved standing nearby, he said to her, "Woman, here is your son," and to the disciple, "Here is your mother." From that time on, this disciple took her into his home. Later, knowing that everything had now been finished, and so that the Scripture would be fulfilled, Jesus said, "I am thirsty." A jar of wine vinegar was there, so they soaked a sponge in it, put the sponge on a stalk of the hyssop plant, and lifted it to Jesus lips. When he had received the drink, Jesus said, "It is finished." With*** *that, he bowed his head and gave up his spirit'* – John 19:25-30, you will discover by the revealed revelations that it too, is a deceptive trap! For example: **Mary** the mother of Jesus *(as corresponding to the elder sister Martha)* and **Mary Magdalene** *(as corresponding to the younger sister Mary)* was never at the crucifixion as revealed by this description *'for the place where Jesus was crucified was near the city'* – John 19:20. Example2: The place where Jesus was supposedly crucified *(near the region city, Jerusalem the Holy City)* can only correspond to one of two regions that reside outside Jerusalem, the Holy City. One of the region's represents the region called Bethany *(borders the land of Egypt)*. The other represents the region called Judea *(Judea's hill region borders the 1ˢᵗ district of Galilee, the region called Nazareth, in the eastern hill country, the land of Samaria)*. If you examine the previous revelations, you will discover that the crucifixion never took place in either of the two regions of the western hill country that reside outside of Jerusalem, the Holy City. This means, it never took place in the land of Jerusalem. Therefore, Martha the Gadarene who corresponds to Mary *(the mother of Jesus)*, and Mary the Gadarene who corresponds to Mary Magdalene, natives of the eastern hill country, the land of Samaria, never resided in the region called Bethany. Thus, Martha and Mary the Gadarenes, were never natives of the western hill country, the land of Jerusalem and the crucifixion never took place in the region of Bethany *(near the Holy City)*, nor in the region of Judea *(near the Holy City)*. This revelation will be revealed in more detail momentarily}

{**Important note4:** This description *'man from the town'* reveals another great deception! For example: Judas the Gadarene, is not called 'the man from the town' but is known as the 'man from the village!' As revealed previously, the town refers to the town called Sychar *(northeast region of the valley, the west bank region of the Gerasenes)*. Judas the Gadarene, however, resides in the remote village called Ephraim, near the southwest exit gate of Sychar *(leaving the town called Sychar)*. Therefore, the description 'man from the town' is actually 'man from the village.' This revelation corresponds to this description *'This is a remote place (region of the Gadarenes), and it's already getting late. Send the crowds away, so they can go to the villages (village called Ephraim) and buy themselves some food'* – Matthew 14:15. Thus, Judas the Gadarene resides in the vicinity of Tyre *(open field called the open area)* near the northeast entrance gate of Sychar, revealed as the coast of Tyre *(resides near the Foot of the Mountain)*}

The next thing you must do is look closely at the bold portion in the following descriptions below,

Matthew 27:33 - [They came to a **place called Golgotha (which means The Place of the Skull]**

Mark 15:22 - [They brought Jesus to the **place called Golgotha (which means The Place of the Skull)]**

Luke 23:33 - [When they **came to the place called the Skull**, there they crucified him, along with the criminals – one on his right, the other on his left]

John 19:17 - [Carrying his own cross, he **went out to the place of the Skull (which in Aramaic is called Golgotha)]**

Next, remove the following descriptions from the verses.

1- place called Golgotha (which means The Place of the Skull)
2- came to the place called the Skull
3- went out to the place of the Skull (which in Aramaic is called Golgotha)

(Note20: The following descriptions above reveal two major clues. For example: The **'place called Golgotha'** *is symbolic and corresponds to the southwest region of the valley of Sychar, the level terrain section of the valley (also known as the entrance and exit gate). This revelation also corresponds to the bold portion of this description* **'There were entrances to the side rooms from the open area, one on the north and another on the south;** *and the base adjoining the open area was five cubits wide all around' – Ezekiel 41:11))*

(Note21: The **'place of the Skull'** *is also symbolic and corresponds to the bold part of this description 'There were entrances to the side rooms from the open area, one on the north and another on the south;* **and the base adjoining the open area was five cubits wide all around'** *– Ezekiel 41:11. This revelation also corresponds to this description* **'a stone laid across the entrance'** *– John 11:38 (the entrance as corresponding to the northeast entrance gate and the southwest exit gate of Sychar). Therefore, the 'place of the Skull' represents a* **Large Rock** *that separates the northeast region of the valley of Sychar (the coast of Sidon) from the southwest region of the valley of Sychar (the coast of Tyre). This revelation reveals the*

meaning behind this description **'in the valley** *(the valley of Sychar)* **of those who travel east of the Sea** *(northeast entrance gate of Sychar).* **It will block the way of travelers** *(Large Rock that blocks the entrance of the valley, as representing the place of the Skull),* **because Gog and all his hordes will be buried there** *(level terrain section of the valley, as representing the place called Golgotha).* **So it will be called the Valley of Hamon Gog** *(southwest region of the valley of Sychar)'* - *Ezekiel 39:11. This revelation fulfills the meaning behind this description* **"What is that tombstone I see?"** *(The base adjoining the open area) –* *2ⁿᵈ Kings 23:17))*

Here are the final revelations: **'The place which in Aramaic that is called Golgotha'** corresponds to the southwest region of the valley of Sychar and represents the following place: [The coast of Tyre *(level terrain section of the valley)*].

… And…

The **'place of the Skull'** represents a large Rock that blocks the entrance of the valley and corresponds to the 'base adjoining the open area *(five cubits wide all around)*' as representing the following place: [The Foot of the Mountain *(also known as the tombstone shaped mountain)*].

(Note22: The Foot of the Mountain will be revealed in more detail throughout the 3ʳᵈ Chronicle series of the Elijah Doctrine)

{**Important note5:** If you look closely at the description of the verses: **'Finally Pilate handed him over to them to be crucified. So the soldiers took charge of Jesus. Carrying his own cross, he went out to the place of the Skull (which in Aramaic is called Golgotha)'** – John 19:16-17, you will discover by the revealed revelations that it is another deceptive trap! For example: As previously revealed, the two regions outside of Jerusalem the Holy City represents the regions known as the region of Bethany *(less than two miles from Jerusalem the Holy City, borders the land of Egypt)*, and the region of Judea *(Judea's hill region borders the region of the eastern hill country, the 1ˢᵗ district of Galilee, the region of Nazareth)*. The place in Aramaic called Golgotha is not located in either of the two regions that reside outside of Jerusalem the Holy City. As previously revealed, the place called Golgotha *(which means The Place of the Skull)* is not located in the land of the western hill country, the land of Jerusalem. It is in the land of the eastern hill country, the land of Samaria, where the place called Golgotha *(level terrain section of the valley)*, and the place of the Skull *(Foot of the Mountain)* is located. Thus, proving the following verse **'for the place where Jesus was crucified was near the city'** – John 19:20, to be a deceptive trap! The place called Golgotha does not correspond to Jesus *(having been crucified)* but corresponds to John the Levite *(having been beheaded)*. It was John the Levite *(Man of God who came from Judah)*, who was buried at the place called Golgotha *(level terrain section of the valley)*. This area, corresponds to the description **'was near the city.'** The city corresponds to the city called Shechem *(northeast region of the valley of Sychar)*, not Jerusalem the Holy City. This revelation corresponds to the following description **'The people of the city** *(east bank region of the Gerasenes, the city called Shechem)* **said, "It marks the tomb of the man of God who came from Judah'** *(the land of Jerusalem)* – 2nd Kings 23:17. Therefore, the place called the Skull *(which in Aramaic is called Golgotha)*, corresponds to the southwest region of the valley of Sychar *(Foot of the Mountain)* and represents the tomb of John the Levite. This revelation reveals the meaning behind this description **'The king** *(king Herod)* **asked, "What is that tombstone I see?"** *(Large Rock that blocks the entrance of the valley)*}

{**Important note6:** If you look closely at this description **'Taking Jesus body, the two of them wrapped it, with the spices, in strips of linen. This was in accordance with Jewish burial customs. At the place where Jesus was crucified, there was a garden, and in the garden a new tomb, in which no one had ever been laid. Because it was the Jewish day of Preparation and since the tomb was nearby, they laid Jesus there.'** – John 19:40-42, you will discover yet another deceptive trap! For example: As previously revealed, Jesus was raised in the custom of the Gentiles *(though also called a Nazarene, a Galilean and a Samaritan)*. Therefore, Jesus would not have taken a Jewish burial, as is the custom of the Jews, but would have undertaken a burial in the custom of the Gentiles. Example2: The place where Jesus is said to have been crucified *(Golgotha, the place of the Skull)* does not reside in the land of the western hill country, the land of the Jews. Golgotha as corresponding to the level terrain section of the valley, corresponds to this description **'there was a garden, and in the garden a new tomb'** – *John 19:41*. The garden of the tomb corresponds to this description **'the plot of ground Jacob had given to his son Joseph** – John 4:1-7. Thus, the garden is located directly in front of the Foot of the Mountain, which represents a large Rock that blocks the entrance of the valley *(the place of the Skull)*, on the southwest region of the valley of Sychar, the level terrain section of the valley *(The place which in Aramaic that is called Golgotha)*. This revelation reveals the meaning behind this description **'The LORD will surely comfort Zion** *(land of the eastern hill country, land of Samaria)* **and will look with compassion on all her ruins; he will make her deserts like Eden** *(northeast region of the valley of Sychar, the coast of Sidon)*, **her wastelands like the garden of the LORD'** *(southwest region of the valley of Sychar, the coast of Tyre)* – Isaiah 51:3}

Congratulations! You have successfully revealed the 5th and 6th woes hidden behind the 5th and 6th miraculous signs:

..... Jesus never raised Lazarus from the tomb; but was led from the tomb to the open field, called the open area, to the native village of Judas and his sisters, Martha and Mary the Gadarenes *(gathered at the village called Ephraim, the vicinity of Tyre)* **.....**

..... Jesus was never Crucified and placed in a new cut out tomb on the mountain; but mourned with his companions over the detest killing of his relative John the son of Zechariah *(the Man of God who came from Judah)***, who was buried at the place, which in Aramaic that is called Golgotha** *(level terrain section of the valley)***, on the Foot of the Mountain, the place of the Skull** *(the coast of Tyre)*.....

CHAPTER FIVE- 2ND PHASE OF THE CRYPTEX PUZZLE- THE PATH OF THE SIGN

The seventh test in this Chapter is to unveil the mystery revealed behind the [7th woe] by revealing the revelation concealed behind the 7th miraculous sign: [**Jesus walks on water**]!

(Note: In this chapter, you must continue to follow the Path of Judas the Gadarene as he leads Jesus and his companions from the remote village of Ephraim)

THE PATH OF JUDAS THE GADARENE

The next thing you must do is look closely at the bold portion in the following descriptions of Luke 8:37-38 below,

[Then all the people of the region of the Gerasenes asked Jesus to leave them, because they were overcome with fear. **So he got into the boat and left. The man from whom the demons had gone out begged to go with him**, but **Jesus sent him away, saying, "Return home** and tell how much God has done for you]

Next, remove the following descriptions from the verses.

1- So he got into the boat and left
2- The man from whom the demons had gone out begged to go with him
3- Jesus sent him away, saying, "Return home

Next, relist the following descriptions removed from the verses.

- [The man from whom the demons had gone out begged to go with him]
- [Jesus sent him away, saying, "Return home]

(Note2: The following descriptions above reveal a major clue. For example: The man from whom the demons had gone out corresponds to the demon-possessed man from the town, revealed as Judas the Gadarene (the man from the village). Thus, after leaving the village called Ephraim, the home of Martha and Mary the Gadarenes (the vicinity of Tyre), Judas led Jesus and his companions back to the shore region of Gennesaret (where the boats had anchored). Example2: The following description 'begged to go with him' corresponds to this description 'sent him away, saying, return home' (Thus, Jesus instructs Judas the Gadarene to return home to the village of his sisters Martha and Mary the Gadarenes)

{**Important note:** The return of Judas the Gadarene, to the village of his sisters, the village called Ephraim, ends the Path of Judas the Gadarene. Here, you must now follow the Path of Jesus as he and his companions prepare to leave the region of the Gadarenes. This revelation will correspond to this description **(1- So he got into the boat and left)**. This revelation will be revealed in detail shortly}

THE PATH OF JESUS

The next thing you must do is look closely at the bold portion in the following descriptions below,

Matthew 8:24 - [Then he got into the boat and his disciples followed him. **Without warning, a furious storm came up on the lake, so that the waves swept over the boat. But Jesus was sleeping]**

Mark 4:37 - [**A furious squall came up, and the waves broke over the boat, so that it was nearly swamped]**

Mark 6:46 - [Immediately Jesus made his disciples get into the boat and go on ahead of him to Bethsaida, **while he dismissed the crowd. After leaving them, he went up on a mountainside to pray]**

Matthew 8:18 - [**When Jesus saw the crowd around him**, he gave orders to cross to the other side of the lake]

Matthew 14:22 - [Immediately Jesus made the disciples get into the boat and go on ahead of him to the other side, **while he dismissed the crowd]**

Matthew 14:23-25 - [**After he had dismissed them,** he **went up on a mountainside by himself to pray. When evening came, he was there alone, but the boat was already a considerable distance from land, buffeted by the waves because the wind was against it.** During the fourth watch of the night Jesus went out to them, walking on the lake]

Next, remove the following descriptions from the verses.

4- a furious storm came up on the lake, so that the waves swept over the boat

5- Leaving the crowd behind

6- A furious squall came up, and the waves broke over the boat

7- he went up on a mountainside to pray

8- After he had dismissed them

9- went up on a mountainside by himself to pray

10- When evening came, he was there alone, but the boat was already a considerable distance from land, buffeted by the waves because the wind was against it

11- while he dismissed the crowd

12- When Jesus saw the crowd around him

13- while he dismissed the crowd

Next, re-list the following descriptions removed from the verses.

- [a furious storm came up on the lake, so that the waves swept over the boat]
- [A furious squall came up, and the waves broke over the boat]

*(Note3: The two descriptions above reveal another major clue. For example: The following description 'a furious storm' and 'a furious squall' corresponds to the following setting of the day, the late evening. Example2: The furious storm or furious squall represents the hours after 11:00 p.m. The time that Jesus and his companions arrived across the Sea of Galilee to the 4th district of Galilee, to the region of the Gadarenes, corresponds to the time of 11:00 p.m. Thus, the distance between the two lands, **Bethsaida** (set out from the shore region in the evening at 10:00 p.m.) and **Gennesaret** (returned to the shore region and landed at 11:00 p.m.) is proximally one hour by boat. The high tides correspond to the fourth watch of night (representing a furious storm or furious squall) and corresponds between the following time of day: 11:00 to 12:00 p.m., (thus, the earth's gravitational pull also brings the high tides during the late evening hours of the day). This revelation corresponds to the bold part of this description 'the boat was already a considerable distance from land, __buffeted by the waves because the wind was against it__' – Matthew 14:24. However, Jesus and his companions having arrived in the region of the Gadarenes at 11:00, would have arrived before the furious storm or furious squall (Thus, the wind would not have been against them; but*

rather, propelling them because the wind would be behind them, not in front of them). This revelation will be revealed in more detail moving forward))

*(Note4: The setting of the day when Jesus and his companions boards the boats to set out from the region of the Gadarenes, the shore region of Gennesaret, does not correspond to the late evening (after the 11ᵗʰ hour) but corresponds to this description '**<u>At daybreak</u>, Jesus went out to a solitary place'** – Luke 4:42 (The solitary place as corresponding to the place where the boats had anchored having returned to the shore region of the 4ᵗʰ district of Galilee at the 11ᵗʰ hour). This area as previously revealed is also known as the region of the Gadarenes (a remote region). Thus, the following words 'a solitary place' (shore region of Gennesaret) corresponds to the words 'a remote region' (region of the Gadarenes). It is during **daybreak** when Judas the Gadarene leads Jesus and his companions back to the solitary place revealed as the shore region of Gennesaret, the place where the two boats had anchored. Therefore, during daybreak the seas would correspond to the term "calm seas" not "rough seas." This revelation reveals the meaning behind the bold portion of this description 'Moses stretched out his hand over the sea, **and at daybreak the sea went back to its place'** – Exodus 14:27. This revelation will be revealed in more detail shortly)*

Here is the next clue: Jesus and his companions leaves the village called Ephraim and returned to the shore region of Gennesaret during the following setting of the day: [Daybreak *(as representing sunrise, also called 'dawn' or the 'break of day')*].

Next, re-list the following descriptions removed from the verses. Take careful note to the bold words of the descriptions below,

- [**Leaving** the crowd behind]
- [After he had **dismissed** them]
- [while he **dismissed** the crowd]
- [while he **dismissed** the crowd]

(Note5: The following descriptions above reveals another hidden clue. For example: The word 'dismissed' corresponds to the following description 'Jesus sent him away, saying, "Return home' (thus, Jesus does not dismiss the crowd, known as the Gerasenes). On the contrary, he only dismisses Judas the Gadarene. If you recall, the people of the town, representing the town called Sychar (west bank region of the Gerasenes) begged them to leave their region (as representing the northeast region of the valley of Sychar). Therefore, Jesus and his companions do not return to the northeast region of the valley of Sychar to dismiss the crowd))

Next, re-list the following descriptions removed from the verses.

- [he went up on a mountainside to pray]
- [went up on a mountainside by himself to pray]

(Note6: The following descriptions above also reveals another hidden clue. For example: The mountainside corresponds to the southside of the Mountain (the Mountain of the south). This area refers to the 'coast of Tyre' (also known as the southwest region of the valley of Sychar). The mountainside corresponds to the following description 'the base adjoining the open area' (also known as the tombstone shaped mountain). Thus, Jesus does not go up on the mountainside to pray, nor does he go alone, but is led by Judas the Gadarene to the level terrain section of the valley to bury his relative John the son of Zechariah, also known as John the Levite (the Man of God who came from Judah) on the Foot of the Mountain (large Rock that blocks the entrance of the valley))

The next thing you must do is look closely at the bold portion in the following descriptions below,

Matthew 14:23-25 – [After he had dismissed them, he went up on a mountainside by himself to pray. **When evening came, he was there alone, but the boat was already a considerable distance from land, buffeted by the waves because the wind was against it. During the fourth watch of the night Jesus went out to them, walking on the lake]**

Mark 6:47-48 – [**When evening came, the boat was in the middle of the lake, and he was alone on land. He saw the disciples straining at the oars, because the wind was against them. About the fourth watch of the night he went out to them, walking on the lake]**

Next, remove the following descriptions from the verses.

10- During the fourth watch of the night Jesus went out to them, walking on the lake
11- When evening came, the boat was in the middle of the lake, and he was alone on land
12- He saw the disciples straining at the oars, because the wind was against them.
13- About the fourth watch of the night he went out to them, walking on the lake

(Note7: The following descriptions above also reveal another hidden clue. For example: The fourth watch of night is symbolic and corresponds to the hours after the 11th hour. If you recall, Jesus and his companions returned to the shore region of Gennesaret during the 11th hour (meant Judas the Gadarene in the evening of day, in the region of the Gadarenes). Thus, the 'fourth watch of night' corresponds to the following hours of the day, 'mid night' and corresponds to the approximate time of day between the hours of 11:00 p.m. and 12:00 a.m. Thus, Jesus and his companions do not leave the shore region of Gennesaret during the late hours of the day (rough seas), but leaves the region during the hours of daybreak (calm seas))

{**Important note2:** If you look closely at the description of the two verses, *'Shortly before dawn Jesus went out to them, walking on the lake'* – Matthew 14:25, and *'Then Peter got down out of the boat, walked on the water and came toward Jesus. But when he saw the wind, he was afraid and, beginning to sink, cried out, "Lord, save me!"'* – Matthew 14:29-30, you will discover it is another deceptive trap! For example: If you look closely at these descriptions *'Shortly before dawn'* and *'he saw the wind,'* you will discover the wind would not be a factor during the hours of dawn *(as representing daybreak)*. Thus, no wind would have been blowing in an alarming way to signify rough seas. This revelation corresponds to the

178

following verse, *'Moses stretched out his hand over the sea, <u>and at daybreak the sea went back to its</u>* <u>*place'*</u> – Exodus 14:27}

{**Important note3:** If you look closely at the description of the following verses, *'When evening came, his disciples went down to the lake, where they got into a boat and set off across the lake for Capernaum. By now it was dark, and Jesus had not yet joined them. A strong wind was blowing and the waters grew rough'* – John 6:16-19, you will discover that it too, is a deceptive trap! For example: Jesus only passed through the 2ⁿᵈ district of Galilee, the district region called Capernaum to reach the 3ʳᵈ district of Galilee, the district region called Bethsaida. Thus, Jesus and his companions never sailed to the Jordan River from the region of Gennesaret, nor did Jesus and his companions journey to the region of Capernaum from the region of Bethsaida. As previously revealed, they only journeyed across the Sea of Galilee to the 4ᵗʰ district of Galilee, the region called Gennesaret. Example2: Jesus and his companions left the shore region of Bethsaida during the 10ᵗʰ hour *(evening of the day)* from the 3ʳᵈ district of Galilee, the region called Bethsaida and returned to the 4ᵗʰ district of Galilee, the region called Gennesaret at 11:00 p.m. *(not Capernaum)*. Example4: These revelations reveal how Jesus not only left the shore region of Bethsaida by boat *(late evening of the day)*, but also, reveals how Jesus left the shore region of Gennesaret by boat *(hours of daybreak)*. This revelation will be revealed in more detail shortly}

{**Important note4:** If you look closely at the description of the verse, *'Then he got into the boat and his disciples followed him'* – Matthew 8:23, you will discover a clue that reveals how Jesus, and his companions *(two boats)* left the region of the Gadarenes, the shore region called Gennesaret, at daybreak. If you look closely at this description *'Suddenly a furious storm came up on the lake, so that the waves swept over the boat. But Jesus was sleeping. The disciples went and woke him, saying, "Lord, save us! We're going to drown!" He replied, "You of little faith, why are you so afraid?" Then he got up and rebuked the winds and the waves, and it was completely calm'* – Matthew 8:24-26, you will discover a clue, visible in plain sight! For example: If you look again at this description *'rebuked the winds and the waves, and it was completely calm'* you will discover the clue. Example2: This revealing clue is symbolic and confirms how Jesus and his companions did not leave the shore region of Gennesaret during the rough seas *(fourth watch of night)*. This revelation is revealed by this description **<u>'rebuked the winds and the waves!</u>'** This clue reveals they left the region during the hour of daybreak *(calm seas)*. This revelation is revealed by this description **<u>'and it was completely calm!'</u>**}

The next thing you must do is look closely at the bold portion in the following descriptions below,

Matthew 9:1 - [**Jesus stepped into a boat, crossed over and came to his own town**]

Matthew 8:23 - [**Then he got into the boat and his disciples followed him**]

Mark 6:45 - [**Immediately Jesus made his disciples get into the boat and go on ahead of him to Bethsaida**, while he dismissed the crowd]

Matthew 8:18 - [When Jesus saw the crowd around him, **he gave orders to cross to the other side of the lake**]

Matthew 14:22 - [**Immediately Jesus made the disciples get into the boat and go on ahead of him to the other side, while he dismissed the crowd**]

Next, remove the following descriptions from the verses.

14- Jesus stepped into a boat, crossed over and came to his own town
15- Then he got into the boat and his disciples followed him
16- Immediately Jesus made his disciples get into the boat and go on ahead of him to Bethsaida
17- he gave orders to cross to the other side of the lake
18- Immediately Jesus made the disciples get into the boat and go on ahead of him to the other side

Next, re-list the following descriptions removed from the verses.

- [Then he got into the boat and his disciples followed him]
- [Immediately Jesus made his disciples get into the boat and go on ahead of him to Bethsaida]
- [he gave orders to cross to the other side of the lake]
- [Immediately Jesus made the disciples get into the boat and go on ahead of him to the other side]

(Note8: The following descriptions above reveal another major clue. For example: The other side of the Sea of Galilee corresponds to the 3rd district of Galilee, also known as the Bethsaida shore region (the native region of Philip, Nathanael, Simon, Andrew, James, John, Zacchaeus and Levi). Thus, the bold portion of this description 'Jesus stepped into a boat, crossed over and came to his own town' is symbolic and corresponds to the region of Bethsaida, the native district of his companions)

{**Important note5**: The boats do not arrive in the region of Nazareth, Jesus native district, the 1st district called Nazareth. For example: There are only three districts of Galilee that are located near a body of water: These regions are as follows: The Sea of Galilee is in the 3rd and 4th districts of Galilee, called the district region of Bethsaida and the district region of Gennesaret *(the way to the sea – Matthew 4:15)*. The Jordan River is in the 2nd district of Galilee, the district region called Capernaum *(along the Jordan – Matthew 4:15)*. The 1st district of Nazareth borders a hill region land of the western hill country, known as the hill region of Judea. These two region lands, the hill region of Judea *(region in the land of Jerusalem)* and the 1st district of Galilee, called Nazareth *(region in the land of Samaria)* represent what is called the rural areas. This revelation reveals the meaning behind this description **'Nazareth! Can anything good come from there?'** – John 1:46. Therefore, the 1st district of Galilee, the district region called Nazareth, does not reside near a body of water *(the rural area)*}

{**Important note6:** If you look closely at the following two descriptions of the verses, **'When they had rowed some distance away, they saw Jesus approaching the boat, walking on the water; and they were frightened'** – John 6:19 and **'Shortly before dawn Jesus went out to them, walking on the lake. When the disciples saw him walking on the lake, they were terrified. "It's a ghost," they said, and cried out in fear'** – Matthew 14:25, you will discover, it too, is a deceptive trap! For example: At no time did the two boats leave the region of Bethsaida without Jesus aboard one of the boats. This revelation corresponds to the following two descriptions, **'So they went and saw where he was staying, and spent that day with him. It was about the tenth hour'** – John 1:39, and **'That day when evening came, he said to his disciples, "Let us go over to the other side'** – Matthew 8:28. The two description reveals the meaning behind these two descriptions, **'he arrived at the other side in the region of the Gadarenes'** – Matthew 8:28, and **'When Jesus stepped ashore, he was met by a demon-possessed man from the town'** *(Judas the Gadarene)* – Luke 8:27. These descriptions of the verses reveal how Jesus never walked on water by walking across the Sea of Galilee from the 3rd district of Galilee, the district region of Bethsaida. Example2: If you look closely at the description of this verse, **'Jesus stepped into a boat, crossed over'** – Matthew 9:1, you will discover how Jesus is not attempting to walk across the Sea of Galilee from the shore region of Gennesaret to return to the shore region of Bethsaida by foot! This revelation will also be revealed in more detail shortly}

The next thing you must do is look closely at the bold portion in the following descriptions below,

John 6:23 - [**Then some boats from Tibrias landed near the place where the people had eaten the bread** after the Lord had given thanks]

Mark 8:22 - [**They came to Bethsaida**, and some people brought a blind man and begged Jesus to touch him]

Mark 7:24 - [**Jesus left that place and went to the vicinity of Tyre. He entered a house** and did not want anyone to know it; yet he could not keep his presence secret]

Next, remove the following descriptions from the verses.

1- They came to Bethsaida
2- Then some boats from Tibrias landed near the place where the people had eaten the bread
3- Jesus left that place and went to the vicinity of Tyre. He entered a house

Next, re-list the following description remove the verses.

- [Then some boats from Tibrias landed near the place where the people had eaten the bread]

(Note9: The following description above reveals another major clue. For example: The Tibrias is symbolic and corresponds to the shore region that is opposite the shore region of Bethsaida. This shore region represents the shore region of Gennesaret (as representing the place where they hauled the nets of fish into their boats), also called the Sea of Tiberias. This area corresponds to the following description 'Put out into deep water and let down the nets for a catch' (the shore region of Gennesaret))

Next, re-list the final descriptions removed from the verses.

- [They came to Bethsaida]
- [Jesus left that place and went to the vicinity of Tyre. He entered a house]

(Note10: The following descriptions above also reveals a hidden clue. For example: The vicinity of Tyre does not correspond to the 3rd district of Galilee. The vicinity of Tyre corresponds to the 4th district of Galilee, known as the region of the Gadarenes (Jesus left the vicinity of Tyre when he left the village of Judas, Mary and Martha the Gadarenes, the village called Ephraim). Thus, the description 'They came to Bethsaida' (3rd district of Galilee) represents the return of Jesus and his companions, having sailed back across the Sea of Galilee to the 3rd district of Galilee, the region of Bethsaida))

{**Important note7:** If you look closely at the description of the verses *'The disciples went and did as Jesus had instructed them. They brought the donkey and the colt and placed their cloaks on them for Jesus to sit on. A very large crowd spread their cloaks on the road, while others cut branches from the trees and spread them on the road. The crowds that went ahead of him and those that followed shouted, "Hosanna to the Son of David!" "Blessed is he who comes in the name of the Lord!" "Hosanna in the highest heaven!" When Jesus entered Jerusalem, the whole city was stirred and asked, "Who is this?" The crowds answered, "This is Jesus, the prophet from Nazareth in Galilee'* – Matthew 21:6-11, you will discover by the previous revealed revelations that it too, is a deceptive trap! Jesus the Nazarene, also known as the Galilean, the Samaritan, and the Gentile, along with his nine companion natives of the eastern hill country, never stepped foot in the land of the western hill country, the land of Jerusalem, the land of the Jews. They remained in the land of Israel, the land of Samaria, the land of the Gentiles}

{**Important note8:** If you look closely at the description of the verses, *'Then the devil took him to the holy city and had him stand on the highest point of the temple. "If you are the Son of God," he said, "throw yourself down. For it is written: "He will command his angels concerning you, and they will lift you up in their hands, so that you will not strike your foot against a stone'* – Matthew 4:5-6, you will discover that it too, is another deceptive trap! For example: Not only didn't Jesus enter the land of Jerusalem, he also, never entered the capital region city, Jerusalem the Holy City!}

{**Important note9:** If you look closely at the description of the verses, *'He replied, "As you enter the city, a man carrying a jar of water will meet you. Follow him to the house that he enters, and say to the owner of the house, 'The Teacher asks: Where is the guest room, where I may eat the Passover with my disciples?' He will show you a large room upstairs, all furnished. Make preparations there. They left and found things just as Jesus had told them. So they prepared the Passover. When the hour came, Jesus and his apostles reclined at the table. And he said to them, "I have eagerly desired to eat this Passover with you before I suffer. For I tell you, I will not eat it again until it finds fulfillment in the kingdom of God. After taking the cup, he gave thanks and said, "Take this and divide it among you. For I tell you I will not drink again from the fruit of the vine until the kingdom of God comes"* – Luke 22:10-18, you will discover it too, is a deceptive trap! For example: As previously revealed, Jesus and his companions never entered the land of Jerusalem, nor did they enter the capital region city, Jerusalem the Holy City. Example2: Jesus and his companions never partook in the celebration of the Passover, as is the custom of the Jews. They remained in the land of Samaria and lived in the custom of the Gentiles. This revelation fulfills the meaning behind this description *'For Jews do not associate with Samaritans'* – John 4:9}

The next thing you must do is merge the revelations together into the correct context.

- {Nation of Esau} = {Ten Horns} = [Ten kings = Ten tribes: *(Ephraim, Manasseh, Naphtali, Dan, Asher, Issachar, Zebulon, Simeon, Reuben, and Gad)* = Nation of Ephraim = *who are yet to receive a kingdom of their own* = Kingdom of Samaria = Conquered by the Assyrian Empire = Exodus by the Kushite Empire *(Wadi of Egypt)*] = [2nd Exodus] = {Descendants of Esau} = {Eastern hill country} = {Land of Samaria} = {Land of Israel} = {Land of the Gentiles} = [1st District of Galilee = District region of Nazareth *(Joseph, Mary and Jesus exiled)*] = [2nd District of Galilee = District region of Capernaum *(Land of Zebulun and land of Naphtali, the way to the sea, along the Jordan)*] = [3rd District of Galilee = District region of Bethsaida *(Philip, Nathanael, Simon, Andrew, James, John, Zacchaeus and Levi)* = Bethsaida Shore region of Galilee] = [4th District of Galilee = District region of Gennesaret *(region of Tyre and Sidon)* = Gennesaret Shore region of Galilee *(Sea of Tiberias, and **Tibrias**)*] = [Region of the Gadarenes: *(Caesarea Philippi)* = *(Judas, Mary and Martha the Gadarenes)* = Southwest region of the valley of Sychar = Coast of Tyre *(Foot of the Mountain)* = Vicinity of Tyre = Village called Ephraim *(open field, open area)*] = [Northeast region of the valley of Sychar = Coast of Sidon = Region of the Gerasenes: Town called Sychar *(west bank region)* and Capital region city called Shechem *(east bank region)*]

- {Nation of Jacob} = {Beast} = [single tribe: *(Benjamin)* = Nation of Judah = *remained in the city* = Conquered by Babylonian Empire = Exodus by the Persian Empire] = [2nd Exodus] = [Kingdom of Jerusalem] = {Descendants of Jacob} = {Western hill country} = {Land of Jerusalem} = {Land of the Jews} = [Hill country of Judea: *(Zechariah, Elizabeth and John son of Zechariah)*] = [Region of Judea: *(Joseph and Mary)*] = [Capital region of Jerusalem = Jerusalem the Holy City: *(John becomes a Levite priest before the Temple courts)*] = [Region of Bethany *(less than two miles from Jerusalem the Holy City)*]

Next, re-list the entire descriptions removed from the verses and place the bold descriptions in the correct number order according to the context of the story.

So he got into the boat and left

[94] **The man from whom the demons had gone out begged to go with him**

[95] **Jesus sent him away, saying, "Return home**

[96] **Jesus stepped into a boat**, [100] **crossed over and** came to his own town

Then he got into the boat [98] **and his disciples followed him**

Immediately Jesus made his disciples get into the boat and go on ahead of him to Bethsaida

[97] **he gave orders to cross to the other side** of the lake

Immediately Jesus made the disciples get into the boat and go on ahead of him to the other side

They [102] **Bethsaida**

[99] **Then some boats from Tibrias** [101] **landed** near the place where the people had eaten the bread

[92] **Jesus left that place** and went to [93] **the vicinity of Tyre.** He entered a house

Next, remove the descriptions in the numbered order and construct them into the correct context as seen below,

[92] Jesus left that place [93] the vicinity of Tyre [94] The man from whom the demons had gone out begged to go with him [95] Jesus sent him away, saying, "Return home [96] Jesus stepped into a boat [97] he gave orders to cross to the other side [98] and his disciples followed him [99] Then some boats from Tibrias [100] crossed over and [101] landed [102] Bethsaida

To reveal the final piece to the sacred document of Immanuel you must merge the revelations into the correct context as seen below,

[Leaving Nazareth *(1ˢᵗ district of Galilee)*, he went in Capernaum *(2ⁿᵈ district of Galilee)* Land of Zebulun and land of Naphtali, the way to the sea *(Sea of Galilee)*, along the Jordan *(Jordan River)*] [The next day Jesus decided to leave for the town of Bethsaida *(3ʳᵈ district of Galilee)*] [Now Philip was from Bethsaida, Philip found Nathanael and told him -Jesus of Nazareth, the son of Joseph."][As Jesus walked beside the Sea of Galilee, *(accompanied by Philip and Nathanael)* he saw at the water's edge *(Bethsaida shore region)* two boats, left there by the fishermen *(companions of Philip and Nathanael)*. He saw two brothers - Simon and his brother Andrew, who were washing their nets and asked him to put out a little from shore *(sail beyond the Bethsaida shore region limit)*. He got into one of the boats, the one belonging to Simon *(accompanied by Andrew, Philip and Nathanael)*. Put out into deep water and let down the nets for a catch *(sail to the Gennesaret shore region)*][When he *(Simon)* had gone a little farther, he saw two other brothers, James's son of Zebedee and his brother John *(fishing companions)* in a boat, preparing their nets. Going on from there, *(crossing the Bethsaida border into the Gennesaret region)* his companions *(Simon, Andrew, Philip and Nathanael)* were astonished at the catch of fish they had taken, and so were James and John, the sons of Zebedee *(native companions from the Bethsaida region)* Simon's partners.' So they signaled their partners in the other boat *(James and John -sons of Zebedee)* to come and help them, and they came *(from Bethsaida shore region)* and filled both boats so full that they began to sink *(Gennesaret shore region)*][When the two disciples *(Zacchaeus and Levi the sons of Alphaeus)* heard him say this, they followed Jesus *(returned to Bethsaida)*. Turning around, Jesus saw them following. When the men came to Jesus, they said, "John *(your relative)* sent us to you "where are you staying?" "Come," he replied, "and you will see". So they went and saw where he was staying *(home of Simon and Andrew, the sons of Tanner)*. It was about the tenth hour][That day when evening came *(10:00 p.m.)*, When the sun was setting *(sunset)*, 'When Jesus heard that John had been put in prison he went out of the house *(home of Simon and Andrew the sons of Tanner)*. "Let us go over to the other side" *(Gennesaret shore region)*. That same day they got into the boat set off across the Sea of Galilee, returned to Galilee *(4ᵗʰ district of Galilee)* to a solitary place][Jesus crossed to the far shore of the Sea of Galilee. When he arrived at the other side in the region of the Gadarenes, they landed at Gennesaret and anchored there *(boats of Simon and Andrew, and James and John)*. When Jesus stepped ashore][Jesus got out of the boat a man with an impure spirit came to meet him, he was met by a demon-possessed man from the town *(Judas the Gadarene)*][Jesus went to a town called Nain *(town called Sychar)* he approached the town gate *(northeast entrance gate of Sychar)* a dead person was being carried out *(John the Levite)* a large crowd from the town *(west bank and east bank regions)* of the region of the Gerasene. When they came to Jesus, they saw the man who had been possessed by the legion of demons *(Judas the Gadarene)*. An argument developed on the road *(coast of Sidon)* between some of John's disciples *(Zacchaeus and Levi)* the other disciples, *(Philip, Nathanael, Simon, Andrew, James and John)* they saw a large crowd around them they were afraid. Then the whole town pleaded with Jesus to leave their region *(west bank region of the Gerasenes)*][*(Judas the Gadarene)* led them up a high mountain, *(mountain of the south)* by themselves where they were all alone *(southwest region of the Valley of Sychar)*][Let us put up shelters *(what is that tombstone I see)*. John's disciples came and took his body and buried it *(marks the tomb of the man of God who came from Judah)*. As they were coming down the mountain *(Foot of the Mountain, **place of the Skull**)*. The disciples *(companions)* kept this to themselves. He went down with them and stood on a level place *(level terrain section of the valley, **place called Golgotha**)*][As Jesus and his disciples were on their way, from the tomb a cave with a stone laid across the entrance *(base adjoining the open area)*. At his gate *(northeast entrance gate of Sychar, the coast of Tyre)* he came to a village the village of Mary and her sister Martha *(village called Ephraim)* a woman named Martha opened her home to him. Here a dinner was given in honor *(Man of God who came from Judah)*. Martha and Mary brother served *(grieves over the death of John the Levite)*. While he was reclining at the table. Then Mary poured perfume on Jesus feet with her hair and wiped his feet with her hair *(laments with Jesus over the death of his slain relative John son of Zechariah)*][**Jesus left that place the vicinity of Tyre *(village of Judas, Mary and Martha)*. The man from whom the demons had gone out *(man from the village)* begged to go with him. Jesus sent him away, saying, "Return home *(Village of Ephraim)*. Jesus stepped into a boat *(boat of Simon and Andrew sons of Tanner)* he gave orders to cross to the other side and his disciples *(companions)* followed him *(James and John sons of Zebedee)*. Then some boats from Tibrias *(Gennesaret shore region)* crossed over and landed Bethsaida *(3rd district of Galilee)*]**

{**Important note:** This final piece to the sacred document of Immanuel ends the path of Jesus!}

Congratulations! You have successfully revealed the 7th woe hidden behind the 7th miraculous sign:

….. Jesus never walked on water *(fourth watch of night)*; but left the 4th district of Galilee, the region of the Gadarenes, and sailed from the shore region of Gennesaret, with his companions *(hours of daybreak)* and returned across the Sea of Galilee by boat to the 3rd district of Galilee, the region called Bethsaida …..

In this conclusion, you must reveal the next symbolic sign that surpasses the Sign of Ezekiel. To reveal the revelation of this sign, you must start by locating a hidden clue concealed behind the mystery of Matthew 28:16.

Look closely at the bold portion of the verse in the following description of Matthew 28:16 below,

[**Then the eleven disciples went to Galilee,** to the mountain where Jesus had told them to go]

(Note: This description reveals a major clue. For example: If you look closely at the number of disciples (eleven disciples), you will conclude the number 'eleven' would refer to the death of Judas called Iscariot (hanged himself). Thus, Judas would represent the missing disciple from the twelve chosen disciples bringing the total numbers of disciples to eleven (not accounting for Matthias – Acts 1:26). You would also be wrong! As previously proven, there were never twelve disciples to begin with. As previously revealed, the name Judas called Iscariot is symbolic and corresponds to Judas called the Gadarene (man from the village). Example2: The number 'eleven' is symbolic and corresponds to the time-of-day Jesus and his companions meet Judas the Gadarene, in the region of the Gadarenes (11:00 p.m.))

{**Important note:** There is another clue revealed in the Elijah Doctrine (Revelation of the Sign) that reveals a paradox to Judas the Gadarene, and the time Jesus and his companions arrive in the region of the Gadarenes, at 11:00 p.m.! For example: Judas the Gadarene and 11:00 p.m., corresponds to this description *'which is the name of the beast or the number of its name'* – Revelation 13:17. Example2: The 'name of the beast' *(revealed as Satan)* is symbolic and corresponds to Judas the Gadarene *(demon-possessed man from the town)*, and the 'number of his name' *(4th prominent horn = 4th beast)* corresponds to the time of day, 11:00 p.m. Jesus meets Judas the Gadarene, in the region of the Gadarenes, the district region called Gennesaret *(4th district of Galilee)*}

{**Important note2:** Jesus does not choose twelve disciples at random from different lands or regions. The number of companions Jesus meets from the region of Bethsaida is **'eight'** *(eight natives from the 3rd district of Galilee)*. Jesus the Nazarene, also a native of Galilee *(1st district of Galilee)* brings the number of companions from the same land *(the eastern hill country)* to **'nine'** *(nine Galileans from the land of the Gentiles)*. Thus, Judas the Gadarene, a native from the 4th district of Galilee brings the number of companions to **'ten'** *(ten Samaritans from the land of Samaria)*. This revelation also corresponds to the following description **'I will take the kingdom from his son's hands and give you ten tribes'** – 1st Kings 11:35 *(ten natives representing the descendants of Esau; from the descendant land of Ephraim)*. Thus, all ten companions of Galilee all settled at the home of Judas and his sisters Martha and Mary the Gadarenes in the village of Ephraim *(the vicinity of Tyre)*}

192

{**Important note3:** The 'Man of God' who came from Judah, John the Levite *(the only exile from the land of Jerusalem killed in the land of Samaria who represents a descendant of Judah)*, brings the total number of companions within the land of Israel to **'eleven'** *(eleven companions gathered at the Foot of the Mountain, the coast of Tyre)*. This revelation also corresponds to this description **'I will give one tribe to his son so that David my servant may always have a lamp before me in Jerusalem'** – 1st Kings 11:36 *(thus, representing a native descendant of Jacob; from the descendant line of Judah)*}

*(Note2: The following bold portion of this description 'Then the eleven disciples <u>**went to Galilee**</u>' is symbolic and corresponds to the 4th district of Galilee (the southwest region of the valley of Sychar). This area, also known as the level terrain section of the valley, represents the place where the eleven companions gathered at the **coast of Tyre** (as representing the place called Golgotha). This area represents the place where the eleven companions gathered at the large Rock that blocks the entrance of the valley, as representing the **base adjoining the open area,** revealed as the Foot of the Mountain (as representing the Place called Skull). This revelation corresponds to the following description '"What is that tombstone I see?" – 2nd Kings 23:17. The Foot of the Mountain does not represent the tomb of Lazarus or the tomb of Jesus; but represents the tomb of John the Levite (the only dead companion buried in the land of Samaria who represents a descendant of Judah, and native from the land of the Jews). This revelation corresponds to the following description 'The people of the city said, "It marks the tomb of the man of God who came from Judah' – 2nd Kings 23:17 (the Man of God who came from the land of the western hill country, the land of Jerusalem))*

Here is the final clue: The following description '**Then the eleven disciples went to Galilee**' corresponds to the following companions: ***Jesus, Philip, Nathanael, Simon and Andrew the sons of Tanner, James and John the sons of Zebedee, Zacchaeus and Levi the sons of Alphaeus, Judas the Gadarene and John the Levite*** and represents the following place within the 4th district of Galilee: [The coast of Tyre *(the place called Golgotha)*].

{**Important note4:** If you look at the description of the verses *'When they arrived, they went upstairs to the room where they were staying. Those present were Peter, John, James and Andrew; Philip and Thomas, Bartholomew and Matthew; James son of Alphaeus and Simon the Zealot, and Judas son of James'* – Acts 1:13, you will discover not only is it a deceptive trap but the eleven disciples as depicted in the verses never represented the real companions as was uncovered. The following eleven companions: Jesus, Philip, Nathanael, Simon and Andrew the sons of Tanner, James and John the sons of Zebedee, Zacchaeus and Levi the sons of Alphaeus, Judas the Gadarene and John the Levite, never entered a room in Jerusalem, the Holy City}

{**Important note5:** If you look closely at the two descriptions of the verses, *'Then they cast lots, and the lot fell to Matthias; so he was added to the eleven apostles'* – Acts 1:26, and *'When the day of Pentecost came, they were all together in one place. Suddenly a sound like the blowing of a violent wind came from heaven and filled the whole house where they were sitting. They saw what seemed to be tongues of fire that separated and came to rest on each of them. All of them were filled with the Holy Spirit and began to speak in other tongues as the Spirit enabled them'* – Acts 2:1-4, you will discover they too, are a deceptive trap! For example: If you look again at the previous revealed revelations regarding the following companions: Jesus, Philip, Nathanael, Simon and Andrew the sons of Tanner, James and John the sons of Zebedee, Zacchaeus and Levi the sons of Alphaeus, Judas the Gadarene and John the Levite, you will clearly see how the two verses of Acts, never took place! This revelation is revealed by the bold part of this description – *'Then the eleven disciples went to Galilee'* (the eleven companions did not go to Jerusalem, the Holy City). This revelation will be revealed in more detail shortly}

Next, look closely at the bold portion of the verse in the same description of Matthew 28:16 below,

[Then the eleven disciples went to Galilee, **to the mountain where Jesus had told them to go**]

(Note3: This description reveals another vital clue. For example: The mountain (known as the mountain of the south) corresponds to the High Mountain located in the 4th district of Galilee. Thus, the following description 'where Jesus had told them to go' corresponds to the place in Aramaic that is called Golgotha (as representing the coast of Tyre), to the Place called Skull (as representing the base adjoining the open area))

Here is the final revelation: The following description '**to the mountain where Jesus had told them to go**' corresponds to the Mountain of the South *(southwest region of the Valley of Sychar)* and represents the following place located at the coast of Tyre: [The Foot of the Mountain *(level terrain section of the valley, the Place called Skull)*].

{**Important note6:** The revelations previously revealed by this description *'to the mountain where Jesus had told them to go,'* reveals how this description, *'On one occasion, while he was eating with them, he gave them this command "Do not leave Jerusalem, but wait for the gift my Father promised, which you have heard me speak about. For John baptized with water, but in a few days you will be baptized with the Holy Spirit'* – Acts 1:4-5, is another deceptive trap! For example: The following ten companions: 'Jesus, Philip, Nathanael, Simon and Andrew the sons of Tanner, James and John the sons of Zebedee, Zacchaeus and Levi the sons of Alphaeus, and Judas the Gadarene' never entered the land of the western hill country, the land of Jerusalem, nor did they ever enter the capital region city, Jerusalem the Holy City! The only man from the land of Jerusalem, John the Levite, is proven to be the only native from the eleven companions *(though born in the hill region of Judea, the land of Jerusalem)*, to enter the capital region city, Jerusalem the Holy City. Jesus never commanded the following disciples: 'Peter, John, James and Andrew; Philip and Thomas, Bartholomew and Matthew; James son of Alphaeus and Simon the Zealot, and Judas son of James' because they do not represent the true natives from the land of the eastern hill country, the land of Samaria. Therefore, this description *'Then the apostles returned to Jerusalem from the hill called the Mount of Olives, a Sabbath day's walk from the city'* – Acts 1:12, is proof of another deceptive trap! The ten natives from the eastern hill country, the land of Samaria, never entered the land of Jerusalem}

195

195

THE BIRTH OF THE NEXT GREAT SIGN

The next thing you must do is look closely at the following description of Ezekiel 11:13 below,

[The glory of the Lord went up from within the city and stopped above the mountain east of it]

*(Note4: The 'glory of the Lord' is symbolic and corresponds to the 'Sun!' The bold portion of this description 'went up from within the city **and stopped**' is also symbolic and corresponds to the changing of the next solstice period (known as the end of the winter solstice). This revelation corresponds to the bold portion of this description 'Now the earth was formless and empty, darkness was over the surface of the deep, **and the Spirit of God was hovering over the waters**' – Genesis 1:1-2 (this solstice change will appear in the tropic of Cancer). To reveal this revelation in more detail you must locate another set of hidden clues found in the book of Genesis 1:1-31)*

Look closely at the bold portion in the following descriptions below,

1 In the beginning God created the heavens and the earth. [2] Now the earth was formless and empty, darkness was over the surface of the deep, and the Spirit of God was hovering over the waters. [3] And God said, "Let there be light," and there was light. [4] God saw that the light was good, and he separated the light from the darkness. [5] God called the light "day," and the darkness he called "night." **And there was evening, and there was morning—the first day**.

[6] And God said, "Let there be a vault between the waters to separate water from water." [7] So God made the vault and separated the water under the vault from the water above it. And it was so. [8] God called the vault "sky." **And there was evening, and there was morning—the second day**.

[9] And God said, "Let the water under the sky be gathered to one place, and let dry ground appear." And it was so. [10] God called the dry ground "land," and the gathered waters he called "seas." And God saw that it was good.

[11] Then God said, "Let the land produce vegetation: seed-bearing plants and trees on the land that bear fruit with seed in it, according to their various kinds." And it was so. [12] The land produced vegetation: plants bearing seed according to their kinds and trees bearing fruit with seed in it according to their kinds. **And God saw that it was good. [13] And there was evening, and there was morning—the third day**.

[14] And God said, "Let there be lights in the vault of the sky to separate the day from the night, and let them serve as signs to mark sacred times, and days and years, [15] and let them be lights in the vault of the sky to give light on the earth." And it was so. [16] God made two great lights—the greater light to govern the day and the lesser light to govern the night. He also made the stars. [17] God set them in the vault of the sky to give light on the earth, [18] to govern the day and the night, and to separate light from darkness. And God saw that it was good. [19] **And there was evening, and there was morning—the fourth day**.

[20] And God said, "Let the water teem with living creatures, and let birds fly above the earth across the vault of the sky." [21] So God created the great creatures of the sea and every living thing with which the water teems and that moves about in it, according to their kinds, and every winged bird according to its kind. And God saw that it was good. [22] God blessed them and said, "Be fruitful and increase in number and fill the water in the seas, and let the birds increase on the earth." [23] **And there was evening, and there was morning—the fifth day.**

[31] God saw all that he had made, and it was very good. **And there was evening, and there was morning—the sixth day.**

Next, remove the bold descriptions from the verses and place them in numbered order below,

1- And there was evening, and there was morning—the first day.

2- And there was evening, and there was morning—the second day.

3- And God saw that it was good. And there was evening, and there was morning—the third day.

4- And there was evening, and there was morning—the fourth day.

5- And there was evening, and there was morning—the fifth day.

6- And there was evening, and there was morning—the sixth day.

(Note5: There are two major clues revealed in each of the six descriptions above. For example: The first clue is revealed behind the understanding of the following description 'And there was evening, and there was morning.' Example2: The second clue is revealed behind the revelation of what the six days represent)

Next, separate the descriptions of Genesis by bolding the first part of the descriptions below,

- **And there was evening, and there was morning**—the first day
- **And there was evening, and there was morning**—the second day
- **And there was evening, and there was morning**—the third day
- **And there was evening, and there was morning**—the fourth day
- **And there was evening, and there was morning**—the fifth day
- **And there was evening, and there was morning**—the sixth day

(Note6: If you look closely at the bold descriptions above, you will notice the hidden clue. For example: this description 'there was evening, and there was morning' is symbolic and corresponds to a particular solstice born in the northern hemisphere. Thus, during this solstice there will be sunset (And there was evening); then sunrise (and there was morning))

Here is the 1st clue: The following description *(there was evening, and there was morning)* corresponds to *(there will be sunset then sunrise)* and represents the following solstice period: **[The winter Solstice].**

(Note7: During the winter solstice (which occurs in the northern hemisphere) the Sun will appear to rise again but set in the opposite direction where the Sun would normally set and journey in the opposite direction where there would normally be sunrise. Thus, during the winter solstice as the Sun journeys

across the northern hemisphere, sunset will fall north of true east (thus, there will be evening, and there will be morning during the season of winter))

Next, separate the descriptions of Genesis by bolding the second part of the descriptions.

- And there was evening, and there was morning—**the first day**
- And there was evening, and there was morning—**the second day**
- And there was evening, and there was morning—**the third day**
- And there was evening, and there was morning—**the fourth day**
- And there was evening, and there was morning—**the fifth day**
- And there was evening, and there was morning—**the sixth day**

(Note8: The 1ˢᵗ day is symbolic and corresponds to the 1ˢᵗ month and represents the start of the winter solstice, in which winter begins in the northern hemisphere (on December 21ˢᵗ). The 2ⁿᵈ, 3ʳᵈ, 4ᵗʰ and 5ᵗʰ days are also symbolic and correspond to the 2ⁿᵈ, 3ʳᵈ, 4ᵗʰ and 5ᵗʰ months and represent the Sun's journey across the northern hemisphere surpassing the spring equinox, also known as the Vernal equinox. Thus, the 5ᵗʰ month (5ᵗʰ day) represents the month of May. The 6ᵗʰ month (6ᵗʰ day) represents the month of June, in which the winter solstice draws near to its change and will end on June 21ˢᵗ during the period when the Sun **stops***, comes to* **rest,** *or* **hover***. The next clue to understanding this is revealed in the description of Genesis 1:1-2))*

The next thing you must do is look closely at the bold portion of the following description below,

[In the beginning God created the heavens and the earth. ² Now the earth was formless and empty, darkness was over the surface of the deep, **and the Spirit of God was hovering over the waters.]**

*(Note9: This description reveals two hidden clues. For example: The following description 'the Spirit of God' is symbolic and corresponds to the Sun! Example2: The following description **'was hovering over the waters'** is also symbolic and corresponds to the 6ᵗʰ month (6ᵗʰ day) marking the period in which the winter solstice draws near to its end. Thus, the winter solstice will die in the tropic of Cancer, north of true east)*

*(Note10: The perceived death of John the Levite (beheaded) and the perceived death of Jesus (crucified) is also symbolic. For example: The perceived death of John the Levite (dies in the region land of the **north,** as representing the northeast region of the valley of Sychar) as well as the perceived death of Jesus, crucified outside Jerusalem (dies in the land of the **east**, as representing the eastern hill country) are symbolic and corresponds to the tropic of Cancer, **north** of true **east** (as representing the passing of the sign of Ezekiel). Thus, during the changing of the solstice, the Sun will again appear, north of true east (The glory of the Lord went up from within the city and stopped) and will hover or rest over the waters (Sea of Galilee) in the 4ᵗʰ district of Galilee, the region of Gennesaret. Example2: The death and burial place of both men (placed in a new cut-out tomb on the mountain) is also symbolic and corresponds to the **northeast** entrance gate of Sychar, also known as **Golgotha, the place called Skull** (level terrain section of the valley, the Foot of the Mountain))*

Here is the next revelation: The following description 'the mountain where Jesus had told them to go' *(as representing the Foot of the Mountain)* corresponds to 'the place called Skull' *(as representing the level terrain section of the valley)* and correspond to the changing of the solstice **(north of true east)** that will be viewed from the following territory of the **northeast region of the valley of Sychar**: [The territory of Naphtali].

*(Note11: The **territory of Naphtali** corresponds to the northeast region of the Valley of Sychar (The top section of the valley, the rugged terrain level, the coast of Sidon). This revelation corresponds to the bold portion of this description **'Then Moses climbed Mount Nebo** (Mountain of the south) **from the plains of Moab** (the coast of Tyre) **to the top of Pisgah,** (Foot of the Mountain) **across from Jericho** (the coast of Sidon). **There the LORD showed him the whole land-- from Gilead** (level terrain section of the valley as*

representing the leveled terrain) **to Dan** *(middle section of the valley as representing the rough terrain),* **all of Naphtali** *(The top section of the valley, as representing the rugged terrain level),* **the territory of Ephraim and Manasseh,** *(as representing the west and east bank regions)* **all the land of Judah** *(northeast region of the valley of Sychar)* **as far as the Mediterranean Sea**' *(Southwest region of the valley of Sychar). These territories will be revealed in more detail throughout the 3rd Chronicle series of the Elijah doctrine))*

(Note12: The **mountain of Mount Nebo** *(Moses died and was buried) and the* **mountain of Mount Hor** *(Aaron died and was buried) as well as the* **High Mountain** *(John the Levite died and was buried) are all symbolic and corresponds to* **Mount Ebal** *(The Mountain of the South). Thus, they all were buried on the same tombstone shaped mountain revealed as the Foot of the Mountain. This area represents the coast of Tyre and is located across from the territory of Naphtali (the northeast region of the valley of Sychar, the coast of Sidon). The territory of Naphtali also corresponds to the meaning behind the bold part of this description '***So they set apart Kedesh in Galilee*** (the 4th district of Galilee, the region of Gennesaret)* **in the hill country of Naphtali** *(the northeast region of the valley of Sychar, the top section of the valley, the west bank region of the Gerasenes),* **Shechem in the hill country of Ephraim** *(the northeast region of the valley of Sychar, the top section of the valley, the east bank region of the Gerasenes)' - Joshua 20:7))*

(Note13: This description **'The glory of the Lord went up from within the city'** *(east bank region of the Gerasenes, the city called Shechem), means on June 21st, the Sun will reach its highest point from the northeast region of the valley of Sychar, the coast of Sidon (the top rugged terrain section of the valley, the territory of Naphtali). And this description* **'and stopped'** *means the Sun will travel towards the southwest region of the valley of Sychar (revealed as the Western Foothills) and will come to hover in the region of the Gadarenes over the waters of the Sea of Galilee. Thus, the Sun will appear to stop and hover in the 4th district of Galilee (the shore region of Gennesaret) before it appears to reverse in the opposite direction!)*

The next thing you must do is look closely at the bold portion of the following description below,

By the seventh day God had finished the work he had been doing; so **on the seventh day he rested from all his work. Then God blessed the seventh day and made it holy,** because on it he rested from all the work of creating that he had done.

Next, remove the bold portion of the verses from the descriptions.

1- By the seventh day God had finished the work he had been doing
2- on the seventh day he rested from all his work
3- Then God blessed the seventh day and made it holy
4- because on it he rested from all the work of creating that he had done

Next, relist the following descriptions remove from the verses.

- on the seventh day he rested from all his work
- because on it he rested from all the work of creating that he had done

*(Note13: These description reveals another clue. For example: The word **'rested'** also corresponds to the reverse of the solstice change. The word **'rested'** corresponds to the following words: **'hovered'** and **'stopped')***

Next, relist the following descriptions remove from the verses.

- By the seventh day God had finished the work he had been doing
- Then God blessed the seventh day and made it holy

*(Note14: These descriptions also reveal another clue. For example: The seventh day is symbolic and corresponds to June 21ˢᵗ as representing the completion of the solstice change. Thus, the Sun will appear to rise again. This revelation also corresponds to this description **'he was taken up before their very eyes, and a cloud hid him from their sight'** – Acts 1:9. This revelation will be revealed in more detail shortly)*

Here is the next clue: The **7th day** is symbolic and corresponds to **June 21st**, and represents the following revelation [Summer solstice is born in the southern hemisphere *(Sun rises and sets to the land of the west)*]

*(Note15: The completion of the solstice change corresponds to this description **'Men of Galilee, why do you stand here looking into the sky? This same Jesus, who has been taken from you into heaven'** – Acts 1:11. For example: This description 'Men of Galilee' is symbolic and corresponds to the 4th district of Galilee, the region of Gennesaret. Example2: The next part of the description 'who has been taken from you into heaven' is also symbolic and corresponds to the completion of the solstice change (Sun rises again). This revelation fulfills the meaning behind the bold part of this description 'After he said this, **<u>he was taken up before their very eyes, and a cloud hid him from their sight</u>'** – Acts 1:9. As the winter solstice ends in the northern hemisphere and as the summer solstice begins in the southern hemisphere, the Sun will again rise in the east and set to the land of the west. Thus, there will once again be sunrise and sunset (there will again be morning, and there will be evening))*

*(Note16: This description **'will come back in the same way you have seen him go into heaven'** – Acts 1:11, is also symbolic and represents the changing of the next solstice as representing the start of the winter solstice (born south of true west, the tropic of Capricorn). Thus, on December 21st Mary will once again give birth to Jesus in the land of the west, the Kushite land of Egypt as representing the following: **'the exact time the star had appeared'** (December 21st), **'until it stopped over the place where the child was'** (solstice reverses) **and 'we saw his star when it rose'** (winter solstice is born in the northern hemisphere). Jesus as representing the Sun, will again journey to the land of the eastern hill country, the land of Israel, the land of Samaria (**The glory of the Lord went up from within the city and stopped**) and will again die in the 4th district of Galilee, the region of Gennesaret (**the Spirit of God was hovering over the waters**). Thus, he will again, rise north of true east (tropic of Cancer) in the land of the eastern hill country, the land of Samaria (**he was taken up before their very eyes, and a cloud hid him from their sight**). The word 'waters' in the description refers to the Sea of Galilee (4th district of Galilee, Gennesaret shore region))*

.

Here is the final clue: The following descriptions *'The glory of the Lord went up from within the city and **<u>stopped</u>'** corresponds to the following description *'the Spirit of God was **<u>hovering</u>** over the waters'* as well as correspond to the description *'on the seventh day he **<u>rested</u>** from all his work'* as representing June 21st (7th day) corresponds to the description **'This same Jesus, who has been taken from you into heaven'** and represents the birth of the following solstice: [The start of the Summer Solstice].

(Note17: After the completion of the solstice the name of another great sign will be fulfilled!)

Here is the Final revelation: The **7th day** as representing **June 21st** corresponds to the following two descriptions ***'This same Jesus, who has been taken from you into heaven'*** and ***'he was taken up before their very eyes, and a cloud hid him from their sight'*** as also representing the **'Start of the Summer Solstice'** represents the fulfillment of the next great Sign that will appear **north of true east**, in the tropic of Cancer: [The Sign of Jonah].

{Important note7: The revelations revealed by the start of the Summer Solstice, fulfills the true meaning behind this description ***"A wicked and adulterous generation looks for a sign, but none will be given it except the sign of Jonah"*** – Matthew 16:4}

Congratulations…! You have successfully revealed the Path of the Sign! You may proceed to the meeting of the Knights Templars!

THE REVEALING OF THE KNIGHTS TEMPLARS

Hugh de Payens was the First Grand Master of the Templar order from 1118 to 1136. According to Templar historians he was born in Troyes, Aube, Champagne-Ardenne, France in 1070. As Grand Master, Hugues de Payens, in responding to the call to action issued by Pope Urban II, he organized the original eight Templar knights to defend pilgrims on the road to the Holy Land, known as Jerusalem. The eight men he organized, including himself, to form the original nine Templars, are said to have been relatives by blood or by marriage. Thus, he brought together eight relatives from the same house or country to form what would become known as the Templar Order.

If you look closely at the revelations revealed throughout this 2nd Chronicle, you will discover a paradox between Hugues de Payens and Jesus the Nazarene. This paradox is revealed in the listed examples below,

Example1:

- Hugues de Payens organized eight relatives from the same house or country.

- Jesus the Nazarene also organized eight companions from the same native region, called Bethsaida, also known as the 3rd district of Galilee *(Philip, Nathanael, Simon, Andrew, James, John, Zacchaeus and Levi).*

Example2:

- Hugues de Payens was born in his native land called Troyes, Aube, Champagne-Ardenne, France in 1070 and died in a foreign land on 1136 in the land of Israel, also known today as the land of Palestine.

- Jesus the Nazarene was born in his native land, the Kushite land of Egypt on December 21st *(the start of the winter solstice is born in the tropic of Capricorn, south of true west)* and died on June 21st in the foreign land of Israel, the 4th district of Galilee, also known as the land of Palestine *(the winter solstice ends in the tropic of Cancer, north of true east).*

Example3:

- The nine original members *(which includes Hughes de Payens himself)* protected and defended pilgrims on the road to the Holy Land, known as the Land of Jerusalem.

- The original nine companions *(which includes Jesus the Nazarene himself)* traveled across the Sea of Galilee to protect and defend the honor of John, son of Zechariah *(his relative)*, also known as John the Levite *(the Man of God who came from Judah)*, also known as the Land of Jerusalem.

Example4:

- The Templar headquarters is said to have been located on the Temple Mount, assigned to them by King Baldwin II of Jerusalem.

- The companions of Galilee gathered at the Foot of the mountain as representing the base adjoining the open area *(the tombstone shaped mountain)*, led there by Judas the Gadarene.

Example5:

- The Templars were charged with heresy, spitting on the Cross and obscene kissing *(also known as engaging in unclean acts)*.

- The nine natives of Galilee, also known as the nine Gentile companions of Galilee, were also considered by the Land of the Jews to be unclean *(also known as the uncircumcised)*.

Here is the final revelation: **The Bible was constructed into three cryptex puzzles by the Knight Templars!!!**

{**Important note8:** The third Chronicle series titled 'The Elijah Doctrine 3 *(The Destination of the Sign)*, will reveal the exact place and methods the Knight Templars used to construct the Holy Bible. This revelation will reveal the exact location to the place, where the true image of the one God, who gave rise to the three pillars of religion will be revealed as well as the true origin of the Holy Grail}

The final thing you must do is bring back the revelations revealed by the base decoder regarding the eight horns and merge the following: **Four districts of Galilee from the land of Samaria, the three region lands of Jerusalem, and the land of Egypt,** into the correct places. As seen below,

- {Two horns *(ram)*} = [two heads = two hills = two kings] = [two stars = two spirits before his throne = 1st and 2nd angels blasting two trumpets] = [1st and 2nd priests *(blowing trumpets)* = horns and sounding of rams = 1st and 2nd men = 1st and 2nd elders of Judah = two golden lampstands] = [{**The Region of Judea:** *(Joseph, Mary, Zechariah, Elizabeth and John son of Zechariah)*} = {The Region of Bethany *(less than two miles from Jerusalem the Holy City)*}]

- {Larger horn *(goat)*} = [third head = third hill = 3RD king] = [3rd star = 3rd spirit before his throne = 3rd angel blasting 3rd trumpet] = [3rd priest *(blowing trumpet)* = trumpets = 3rd man = 3rd elder of Judah = 3rd golden lampstand] = {**Region Capital City: Jerusalem the Holy City: *(The Temple of the Lord)***}

- {1ST prominent horn} = [4TH head = 4TH hill = 4TH king] = [4th star = 4th angel of the seven churches = 4th angel blasting 4th trumpet] = [4th priest *(blowing trumpet)* = Harps = 4th man = 4th elder of Judah] = [4th golden lampstand = 4th church] = [1ST beast = 1ST living creature = 1ST cherubim = 1ST chariot = Brown horses = 1ST spirit = 1ST angel = North = 1st wind of the earth = 1st wind of heaven *(churning up the great sea)* = 1ST guard of the city = 1ST apocalyptic rider *(Its rider held a bow)* = Brown horses = 1ST swift messenger = peals of thunder] = [1ST kingdom of Gold = Element of Gold = Fall of the Egyptian era] = [**1st District of Galilee = District region of Nazareth** *(Joseph, Mary and Jesus exiled)*]

- {2ND prominent horn} = [5TH head = 5TH hill = 5TH king] = [5th star = 5th spirit before his throne = 5th angel blasting 5th trumpet] = [5th priest *(blowing trumpet)* = cymbals = 5th man = 5th elder of Judah = 5th golden lampstand] = [2ND beast = 2ND living creature = 2ND cherubim = 2ND chariot = Black horses = 2ND spirit = 2ND angel = South = 2nd wind of the earth = 2nd wind of heaven *(churning up the great sea)* = 2ND guard of the city = 2ND apocalyptic rider *(Its rider was holding a pair of scales in his hand)* = Black horses = 2ND swift messenger = rumblings] = [2ND kingdom = Element of Silver = Fall of the Babylonian era] = [**2nd District of Galilee = District region of Capernaum** *(Land of Zebulun and land of Naphtali, the way to the sea, along the Jordan)*]

- {3RD prominent horn} = [6TH head = 6TH hill = 6TH king] = [6th star = 6th spirit before his throne = 6th angel blasting 6th trumpet] = [6th priest *(blowing trumpet)* = Lyres = 6th man = 6th elder of Judah = 6th golden lampstand] = [3RD beast = 3RD living creature = 3RD cherubim = 3RD chariot = Pale horses = 3RD spirit = 3RD angel = West = 3rd wind of the earth = 3rd wind of heaven *(churning up the great sea)* = 3RD guard of the city = 3RD apocalyptic rider *(to kill by sword, famine and plague)* = Pale horses = 3RD swift messenger = flashes of lightning] = [3RD kingdom = Element of Bronze = Fall of the Persian era] = **[3rd District of Galilee = District region of Bethsaida *(Philip, Nathanael, Simon, Andrew, James, John, Zacchaeus and Levi)* = Bethsaida Shore region of Galilee]**

- {4TH prominent horn} = [7TH head = 7TH hill = 7TH king] = [7th star = 7th spirit before his throne = 7th angel blasting 7th trumpet] = [7th priest *(blowing trumpet)* = shouts = 7th man = 7th elder of Judah = 7th golden lampstand] = [4TH beast = 4THliving creature = 4THcherubim = 4THchariot = Fiery red horses = 4THspirit = 4THangel = East = 4th wind of the earth = 4th wind of heaven *(churning up the great sea)* = 4TH guard of the city = 4TH apocalyptic rider *(To him was given a large sword)* = Fiery red horses = 4TH swift messenger = earthquake] = [Satan *(name of a man)* = Mighty angel *(coming up from the east)*] = [4th kingdom = Element of Iron = Fall of the Greek era] = **[4th District of Galilee = District region of Gennesaret *(coastal regions of Tyre and Sidon)* = Gennesaret Shore region of Galilee *(Sea of Tiberias and Tibrias)*] = [Region of the Gadarenes: *(Caesarea Philippi)* Southwest region of the valley of Sychar = Coast of Tyre *(Foot of the Mountain)* = Vicinity of Tyre = Village called Ephraim *(Judas, Mary and Martha the Gadarenes)*] = [Northeast region of the valley of Sychar = Coast of Sidon = Region of the Gerasenes: Town called Sychar *(west bank region)* and Capital region city called Shechem *(east bank region)*]**

- [5th prominent horn] = [Solid gold lampstand = Someone like a son of man = Michael = Man clothed in linen (writing kit at his side) = *He came and took the scroll from the right hand of him who sat on the throne! = The armies of heaven were following him, riding on white horses and dressed in fine linen, white and clean = (And from His mouth proceeds a sharp sword)* = 8th king = King of Kings = Lord of Lords = Naphtali] = [5th beast = Woman = Dinah = 5th living creature = Lamb looking as though slain *(will hate the prostitute)* = 5th cherubim = 5th chariot = White horses = 5th angel = 5th guard of the city = 5th apocalyptic rider *(from His mouth proceeds a sharp sword)* = White horses = A great hailstorm] = [twelfth tribe = The tribe of Dinah *= started small but grew in power* = 5th kingdom = Element of Rock = Coming Age] = {Pharaoh Tirhakah *(Pharoah of Egypt)*} = [Empire of Kush] = [Land divided by rivers: *(Blue Nile River)* and *(White Nile River)*] = [a people tall and smooth-skinned, to a people feared far and wide, an aggressive nation of strange speech] = [Invaded the land of Egypt *(Egypt fell in the 25th dynasty)*] = [Invaded the land of Assyria *(captured the Samarian Israelites)*] = [Ancient Nubia *(land of the Kushites)*] = [Western region of upper Egypt = Punt *(Libyans)*] and [Eastern region of upper Egypt = Put *(Nubians)* = The Red Sea *(waters you saw where the prostitute sits)*] = [Queen of the South *(Woman clothed with the sun)* = A great and wondrous sign = 5th spirit = The Sun = The passing of the Sign of Jonah *(summer solstice ends in the southern hemisphere)* = End of the Summer Solstice *(on Dec 21st)*] = {**The Land of Egypt: *(native birth place of Jesus, also known as Emmanuel)*}**

Congratulations! You have proven yourself worthy to possess the second piece of the Grail map. Complete your journey by proceeding to the final page!

Here is the [2nd map coordinates] to reach the ancient city:

- {Start - **[West]** - of the compass line from the Kushite land of Egypt -do- **[East]** – for the ancient land of Palestine, and journey to the southwest region of the valley of Sychar, the level terrain section of the valley, the coast of Tyre *(revealed as Golgotha)* and stand facing the Foot of the Mountain *(revealed as the place called the Skull)*}

Congratulations! You have successfully completed the 2nd Cryptex puzzle! You may proceed to the 3rd Chronicle titled '**The Elijah Doctrine 3_ The Destination of the sign_ Vol-1_Genesis**'

The Elijah Doctrine Chronicles is dedicated to:

My daughters: Yahanna T. Bennett, Elayah P. Bennett and Saharah A. Bennett

My Mother: Olivia Bennett

Special dedication:

To all the free thinkers of the world; past and present!

'We will end this war and redeem the souls of the damned and the lives of the condemned! Together, we will raise to the surface a new world. A world that stands as one people, nation, and languages under one banner to bring to justice the institutions that have perverted our humanity. You shall be set free from the bondage of others who seek to keep your minds captive to the darkness of ignorance, and you shall awaken to the truth of disillusion!'

Elijah H. Bennett

You may continue to the 2nd Chronicle_ **The Elijah Doctrine 3_ The Destination of the sign_ Vol-1_Genesis** …

www.ingramcontent.com/pod-product-compliance
Lightning Source LLC
Chambersburg PA
CBHW080502110426
42742CB00017B/2968